VAN-ISHING POINT

NOT A MEMOIR

OTHER BOOKS BY ANDER MONSON

Nonfiction

Neck Deep and Other Predicaments

Poetry

The Available World
Vacationland

Fiction

Other Electricities

VAN-ISHING POINT

NOT A MEMOIR

Ander Monson

Graywolf Press

Publication of this volume is made possible in part by a grant provided by the Minnesota State Arts Board, through an appropriation by the Minnesota State Legislature; a grant from the Wells Fargo Foundation Minnesota; and a grant from the National Endowment for the Arts, which believes that a great nation deserves great art. Significant support has also been provided by Target; the McKnight Foundation; and other generous contributions from foundations, corporations, and individuals. To these organizations and individuals we offer our heartfelt thanks.

Published by Graywolf Press
250 Third Avenue North, Suite 600
Minneapolis, Minnesota 55401

www.graywolfpress.org

Published in the United States of America

ISBN 978-1-55597-554-8

2 4 6 8 9 7 5 3 1
First Graywolf Printing, 2010

Library of Congress Control Number: 2009933825

Cover design: Kyle G. Hunter

Cover photo: Michael Cook

CONTENTS

for M., a world herself

HOW-TO*†*

The crosslike glyph after "HOW-TO" above is a dagger.*†* The glyph adorning "dagger" just now is also a dagger, only smaller. It is, in this case, and throughout the book,*†* italicized, and in superscript. This is in contrast to the exhortations of *The Chicago Manual of Style,* which would seem to find this intention pointless, like so many of my intentions.

It looks a little like a cross, depending on the font. It is not. Though it might be the shadow of one, like on a decal on the back of a truck.

It is a weapon. It is a typographic symbol. It is both! You can cut paper with it. It does cut through space,*†* of a sort. It cuts into the sentence flow, interrupts it or adjoins it, parks there while it necks with whoever is in the backseat (lucky seat, lucky dagger, lucky reader!).

This book is a book. It is fixed in time, in space, in print, an artifact. Each of these essays is a kind of frozen thinking, a virtual I that you get to inhabit for a little while. Each is a cheapo virtual reality. Each is my brain, or a constructed simulacrum. The real brain, of course, is flux, motion, synapses connecting and reconnecting and thinking exploding everywhere. You wouldn't want to see that. But I hope your thinking, my thinking, all our thinking goes on long after the essays are written, edited, revised, published, read, critiqued, disputed, redacted, disclaimed. So I have deployed daggers for you if you are interested.

Daggers adorn a few words throughout the book. Okay. Each dagger indicates an instance of redirect, a bubbling-over instance, where, for one of many reasons, I have more information, a further reflection, more thinking on the subject that has either gone on past the boundaries of the *object, the fixity* of the book, or is continuing to evolve. Okay, I also have some footnotes and a few endnotes, and some marginalia, but those are in the book. The daggers sometimes lead to things that exceed the capacity of footnotes. Some of them have video. Some images. Some evolving text. I like the web. Its ability to grow and expand and dissolve into clouds and interactions and search strings. So I'm outsourcing these moments to the website† for the book that can surround the book as if it were a candy-coated shell.

These can continue to grow past the book itself. And they do grow, since my brain keeps assembling more structures. These are for me. They are also for you. Think of them, maybe, like extended footnotes. They are optional like footnotes, like desserts, like extra-credit questions, like side quests in the video games I play. If you are interested, go online to the book's website, otherelectricities.com/vp/, and type the word in the box for more content.

Is it kind of clunky? Yes. Is it worth your time? I believe also yes.

It's the best way I can come up with to make this work.

Think about them like you would Choose-Your-Own Adventure books, or like text adventures (also sometimes called *interactive fictions*), or like the afterparty for the book itself with a sweet DJ and more good drinks. If you were reading this on whatever comes after the Kindle, maybe we could make these clickable. But you're not (not yet). This is old but good technology, pressed and dried paper pulp bound by glue in your hands and smelling good, like something real. Maybe the daggers are more like clickable links, like this whole thing is an expanding wiki, an increasingly fat American self growing and thinking and growing, a ball† getting larger and larger the more I think about it, the more you think about it, the more you and I become we and we continue thinking about all of this stuff together.

VOIR DIRE

"Do you solemnly swear that the evidence you are about to give in this matter is the truth, the whole truth, and nothing but the truth?"

Let's start with the facts: three hundred of us, being citizens of this United States, are selected randomly and called to the Kent County Circuit Courthouse, Grand Rapids, Michigan, on a Monday morning. It is drizzly, dreary. I am barely awake and have a poor outlook on the world, which is operating in grayscale. Out of three hundred, thirty of us are called to make up a potential jury for a trial overseen by Judge Redford on the eleventh floor. I am one of the first five. We rise, are asked to turn our cell phones off, and proceed upstairs, where the real action will happen. Of the thirty, I am one of the fourteen randomly selected for the jury, pending voir dire, in which we are asked to answer questions truthfully about our biases and histories. We are seated in the box, quiet, awaiting instructions. There are no snacks allowed.

I didn't expect to be summoned to the courthouse, as I listed my occupation on the form I received in the mail a couple of weeks earlier as writer/journalist. Certainly lawyers, judges, and jury clerks wouldn't want a writer-slash-journalist involved in deliberations of guilt? Said writer might be tempted to try to take notes and make something of the experience— document it, repurpose it, make it about himself. "Journalist," however, is a little bit of a stretch for me, as I wouldn't characterize my writing—even my nonfiction—as journalism, though it does deal in truth, fact, and in verifiable research. As such it perhaps deserves the slash and moniker: its sentences are heavy with actual, demonstrable truth content; the result is not mistakable for memoir. But I am called to the courthouse anyway, and the rhetoric of civic duty as one of the sacred tenets of American law and citizenship means that I am actually not so disappointed. I grew up watching *L.A. Law, Law & Order, The Practice,* and *Perry Mason.* I read some Grisham, have been to court myself under different conditions. I think I want to be chosen. And I am.

Anyone, any given I, any one of you, of y'all, of youse guys (as they say in my hometown), any one of the big mess of us could find ourselves impaneled on a jury. The jury process is a great argument for the education of citizens, particularly using the model of liberal education we endorse at the college where I work. Twelve[1] unrelated people are asked to listen and critically evaluate evidence and witnesses' statements, and then have a rational discussion that leads to a collective agreement on a verdict of guilty or not. This particular gathering represents a flattening, too, of economic and social class, race, gender, and everything else, into citizens— a bunch of people in a small room. We are reduced in this way from individual "I"s to a jury, a "we," an "a." This particular we, this a, this jury, is asked to sit and listen, to deliberate on the matter of the people of the State of Michigan v. Michael Antwone Jordan.[2] This is Case no. 07-0189-FH, and the events described occur July 16–18, 2007. These are helpful facts, verifiable by paper trail. It is late morning. We wait in a windowless and overwarm room. Most of us are hungry. Some of us, surely, are nervous about this responsibility.

I have been thinking about truth and fact a lot lately, outside of this context. Following the acceptance of a piece I wrote for the *Believer* about the Grand Rapids funeral proceedings for former president Gerald R. Ford, I underwent the procedure of fact-checking. Like any medical operation, it was not dignified. The fact-checker wants my notes and collected research, PDFs of press releases. He also wants contact information for my

---

[1] Well, fourteen: two are selected at random at the trial's conclusion as alternates and are not asked to deliberate with the others.

[2] Awesomely, one of the witnesses is asked at one point during the trial, "Do you recognize the name Michael Jordan?"

brother (to check a very minor comment about my brother and his new baby), my father (to fact-check some minor personal history), and a college friend (to verify that I smashed a guitar at an open mic). All of a sudden I am asked to prove statements, or at least summon witnesses for corroboration. Maybe this is journalism, I think. Perhaps prompted by recent obvious embarrassments, standards have laudably been raised. In the past I have been happy to rely on the singular authority of the "I" in nonfiction, the essayistic "I" at once bigger than and subset of the writer, the individual, the citizen. This writer-I has additional powers: it can commit information to the permanent record. It gets to speak, to tell its story. It can pretend it is a monolith. It can control the release and position of facts; if and what to reveal, and when; how self-serving to appear, to be. It can inscribe them on paper in the form of notes. It can answer, be affronted by, or rebut fact-checking queries. It can be wrong. It can be shamed.

The chairs are comfortable, high-tech, crisscrossed by webbing, which likely means expensive—they're similar to the Herman Miller Aeron chair. The chair choice suggests we will be here for a while. We are instructed by the judge to not discuss the case with anyone before its conclusion, which should be in a few days.† Fact: the defendant, Michael Antwone Jordan (MAJ), is charged with two counts of the esoteric charge "uttering and publishing." We on the jury are specifically asked not to research anything possibly relating to the case (no Google, we're told), so we are not subject to outside influence or information. All of what we are allowed to know and act on is to be parsed by the attorneys and the judge.

We are instructed (and later research bears this out) that the charge *uttering and publishing* means the defendant is alleged to have created and presented a false document as real (in this case: two checks, hence two counts). MAJ is alleged to have stolen or otherwise acquired two paychecks not made out to him, and (*uttering*) forged the payee's signature, then adding *Pay To Michael Antwone Jordan*. He then (*publishing*) signed for them and deposited the checks in his bank account. There are other terms for this, I think: Forgery. Plagiarism. Mail or other fraud. Theft. I look at him. He does not look back.

Fact, verifiable according to the *Detroit Free Press* ("2 Youths Accused of Computer Fraud: Teens Broke Secrets of 2 Firms, Police Say"[3]) and the public record: Ander Monson was prosecuted in 1993 for seven counts of felony credit card fraud. He was a minor when arrested, so technically he doesn't have to admit to this conviction on job applications and such, or as part of the voir dire process (which, in this context, is the examination of the jury by the judge and trial lawyers to determine if prospective jurors are competent, and if they have any unwelcome biases toward the matter under consideration). Or at least he is not sure that he is not required to disclose this. The jury clerk, Mrs. Greta Van Timmeren, told the group downstairs that if they weren't sure, they should always disclose. He is therefore fairly sure, but to be positive he would have to ask a lawyer (not one of these lawyers). Fact: Ander Monson chooses not to disclose his criminal past. Supposition: Ander Monson wants to be on this jury. Supposition: Ander Monson's nondisclosure of this initial fact might come back to haunt him. Fact: Ander Monson does not appear to care.[4]

Fact: Several of the details in the *Free Press* story are false (my online identity was not, in fact, "the Black Wizard"), but are presented as utter journalistic truth. One wonders about the quality of their fact-checking. Here is a great line about hacker culture from the article: "Monson is pretty much a loner . . . black kids, white kids, Asians—there is one thing they have in common: they are intelligent, bright kids who just don't know what to do with their strengths."

---

[3] March 27, 1993: A representative (and inaccurate—or at the very least, ridiculously imprecise—on several counts) sentence states: "He called himself the Black Wizard. And though he was only 16, he had the brains, the cunning, and the connections to crack the computer systems of two major financial corporations, police say." The article rather grandiosely pitches this arrest as part of "the latest wave of alleged credit card fraud among suburban [teens]." Conveniently, in order to access this article in their archives, since I have lost my hard copy, I was required to give them my credit card information.

[4] Not quite true: There is a possibility that I was wrong not to disclose, and that by disclosing here I have somehow created a crack in the conviction that might be used to appeal it and possibly to stick it to me, legally. So there is risk—possible real-world consequence—in relating this.

Fact: All fourteen members initially (randomly) selected for MAJ's jury are white. MAJ is black. Almost everyone else present in the court is white. I assume we are all aware of this. One woman's cell phone goes off in the courtroom, and everyone looks at her. As part of the voir dire process, the twitchy, jowly defense attorney, Norman Miller, is questioning and excusing potential jurors, apparently to try to make the jury more racially representative of the diversity of the city.[†] I have seen this tactic on television, so I think I know something about it. He succeeds, and two black women are randomly selected to join us. One of them is Cell Phone Woman. When asked if she could be impartial on the question before the jury, she replies that there is no way she could ever find anyone guilty, ever: she doesn't believe in it. No one believes this; she's too insistent, too obvious, but she sticks to her claim and is excused. Another juror, also black, is selected to take her place.[†] There are no more challenges. So we six men and eight women will make up the jury, and both defense and prosecution agree that everyone remaining is acceptable to all parties. We adjourn for the day. The trial is set to begin tomorrow morning. We are told not to speak to anyone—no family, no spouses, nobody—about any specifics of the trial. We exit, tasked, hushed.

Fact, apparent: At age thirty-two I get a colonoscopy, since my mother[†] died of colon cancer. She was thirty-three. I was seven. I tell my doctor the fact of my mother's death. He recommends this procedure as a wise precaution. He instructs me to make sure the hospital accounting folks process it not as a "screening" (routine) colonoscopy, since those are only covered for those much older than me. They should cover my procedure, though, since my mother died of colon cancer. That's the important fact to make sure I tell them.

When I go in to undergo the procedure I am stocked with dread, even though I'm not going to be conscious for it, or rather, I am told that I will be conscious, but that I will not remember it. What does this do to the idea of a fact if it can't be inscribed in memory?[†] I ask the person who I presume is the anesthesiologist how the amnesia drug they give you works, and she tells me that it disrupts the action of the cerebral cortex, which prevents the mind temporarily from making new memories. This is the last thing I remember.

My wife and the friend who drove me to the procedure relate a number of things I said afterward that I have no memory of saying. Apparently I tried to flash them both, demonstrating the flimsiness of my hospital gown (which had a broken strap: I remember this). This sounds like something I would do, but I don't remember it, as predicted, and this is a little terrifying: both to act without capacity for encoding that action in memory, and to act seemingly unconsciously but in accordance with what I think of as *how I might well act*. I accept that these things occurred, though I have no actual firsthand knowledge of them. I could ask for the photos from the procedure as some sort of evidence. I could interview witnesses. Take some statements.

Fact: We the jury (and anyone called to the witness stand) are asked to take the following oath (if I can be trusted to remember it exactly—or if the judge can, since minor variations are often introduced, according to my notes, each time he speaks it): "do you solemnly swear that the evidence you are about to give in this matter is the truth, the whole truth, and nothing but the truth?" You recognize this from television or movies, I am sure, or think you do. This is a trope we recognize from fictional constructions, and its familiarity is appealing, reassuring. Yes, I know this gig, I think. I feel like I have been here before, in the jury box, because I have seen it dramatized on television. Our collective reliance on fictional constructions is so great that the assistant prosecutor references *CSI* and other forensic television programs as part of her opening statement, in which she talks about the sort of proof and testimony we should expect to see in this trial, and what sort of evidence is sufficient to determine guilt. The process will not be, she warns, as sexy and definitive as it is on TV. I think we know this, that fiction is different than reality, but at the same time we are saturated with fictional representations of courtrooms, of trials, whether compressed and sensationalized on CNN, or on TNT reruns of *Law & Order*. How can we not, on some level, rely on these stories in the absence of actual experience?

The reality of the court process is that it is mostly boring, essentially undramatic—a set of plodding (because thorough), rigid procedures, punctuated by occasional moments of sudden gravity. It mostly surrounds the witnesses, who are obviously uncomfortable on the stand, nervous because they are legally obliged here to tell the truth, the whole truth, and nothing but, and on whose testimony the defendant's future hangs.

Ms. Jan Killiman, assistant prosecuting attorney with the Kent County prosecutor's office and representative of the state, presents her opening statement, invoking the varieties of evidence she is going to present (police statements, witness statements, digital copies of documents, and some original paperwork), thus demonstrating that the prosecution has met what they call their "burden of proof." The defense responds and says that they will show that the prosecution has not met their burden of proof.

Fact, amended: Skip to San Francisco, a couple of weeks after the trial, and I'm informing my brother Ben, his wife, and their new baby of my clean colonoscopy and the grotesque oddity of the procedure. I can't come up with a term other than "procedure," in its technical blankness. Ben asks me why I had a colonoscopy, and I say because of our mother's death from colon cancer, dumbass. He tells me no, she didn't have colon cancer: she died of ovarian cancer, which had spread to her colon, and this is not the same thing. Whoa. I am flummoxed. He is the younger brother, so why does he know this when I do not? I don't even argue, which is rare. In fact, the more I think about it, the less I am sure. I wish I could blame this on the disruption of my cerebral cortex.

This revelation coincides with my realization that the *Believer* fact-checker has found a number of revealing errors in my essay. Some are simple moments where I just chumped it (mistaking the title of the band New Order's first single for the title of their first album, which is minor to most but an unforgivable sin by music-geek standards). Others are more revelatory: my father's explanation that he and my mother did not technically work for the Peace Corps, but "rather [he] worked for the University of Michigan's Center for Research on economic development (CRED), where [he] was assigned to the Ivory Coast (the University of Abidjan) as part of its Francophone African program funded through the U.S. Agency for International Development." Dad later emailed to amend his correction with a second correction from my stepmother that my mother was in fact employed as a staff person at the Ivory Coast headquarters of the Peace Corps when he was teaching at the University of Abidjan.[5] And fact-checking becomes an ongoing process of family discovery.[6]

---

[5] So what I thought to be true turns out to be false, and then true again.

[6] (And of a kind of ritual personal humiliation.)

In MAJ's court case almost every witness called by the prosecution (there are eight or more) has his or her statement attacked by the defense attorney (again, like on TV). Mostly these are quibbles. He asks one victim about the statement that he received paychecks every Friday (as opposed to a particular Friday—the victim claimed to have not been working at this particular temporary job long enough to get more than one paycheck). Another one of the victim's statements conflicts slightly with something on the official police report. The attorney for the defense pursues this, and the witness testimony wobbles slightly. Even the minor witnesses are backed into corners where they make slight mistakes of recall—misremembering a deposit slip as a withdrawal slip, for instance.

Studies do show[7] that eyewitnesses do not remember particularly accurately—not accurately enough, perhaps, for us to value eyewitness testimony over other forms of evidence. We are suggestible, subject to social and psychological pressures, sometimes wrong even though we are sure. This is troubling, especially in the way that we, as "I"s, are made up of memories, millions on millions of minor and major phenomena we witnessed, things that happened to or in front of us. Some of these are easily recalled, and others are activated only occasionally by something as minor as a song, a scent, the memory of vanilla[†] ice cream after a birthday party (if these can be said to be minor, and certainly Proust would demur), a word or voice that we haven't heard in years. And if memories can't be trusted, how can we trust any sense of self at all? Or can something stable emerge from the shaky matrix on which it is based?

I mention this in the jury room later as we deliberate, that this is the most interesting part of the courtroom process to me. We could probably get into some serious philosophy. One of the older gentlemen on the jury laughs and says that's nothing new to him. He forgets things from yesterday, he says, and another older gentleman agrees. There is some cackling. I am young: what do I know about forgetting?

In fact that is a good question: what do we know, and how can we know we know it? We say *we know,* which means we accept a statement to be incontrovertibly true, a fact, unassailable; we have internalized its truth and moved on, built future action and assumption on it. If it turns out to be

---

[7] The standard text on this matter is Elizabeth F. Loftus's *Eyewitness Testimony* (1996), for those who are interested.

false or somehow edited, we are physically changed—synapses rerouted. It means that we trust it; we are not interested in probing its truth content. It becomes part of a story—the stories we tell ourselves about ourselves. Obviously we can't constantly scrutinize everything and test all of our hypotheses, so we trust mainstream sources—scientific journals and magazines that have surely checked these claims out, that have subjected their writers and their claims to fact-checking and double corroboration. We trust consensus, experience, and common sense, as the prosecuting attorney reminds us in voir dire: we can judge what is credible and what is not by the manner in which it is told and the person who tells it.[8]

Fact: As the doctor warned me, it matters to the insurance company whether my mother died of colon cancer. If, according to their algorithms and their battery of claim-checking tests, she did not, then the procedure was technically a screening colonoscopy, and they will not pay for it.[9] Matters are further complicated by the conversation I had with my brother about my mother's actual cause of death (which occurred, notably, after the procedure had been scheduled and completed, and the claim filed). Now that my mother possibly did not die of colon cancer, I am in danger of being again accused of fraud, for claiming my mother died of something she did not and conspiring to get a free colonoscopy.

Fact: For the last several months before the trial I have been reading book-length nonfiction submissions for a national prize. I am the only initial

---

[8] "Say it clearly and you make it beautiful, no matter what" (Bruce Weigl, "The Invisible"). It took me awhile to track down this quote, which I misremembered, interestingly, as "Tell the truth and you make it beautiful, no matter what," which is quite a different idea. In fact, it's nearly the opposite idea. I'm not sure what to make of this misremembering. There is quite a space† between *to tell the truth* and *to say it clearly*. Saying it clearly is saying it beautifully, is being aware of how it is said. In television shows witnesses are prepped for their testimony, to speak clearly and slowly, with no hesitations.

[9] Later in the process of revising this essay I am informed that my insurance claim is indeed denied because they parsed it as preventive, routine, not ordered specifically because of family history. I am currently appealing this decision and assembling evidence in my favor, trying to get to the burden of consumer proof. They assured me prior to the procedure that it would be entirely covered, which was clear, but which did not turn out to be true. So I might be stuck with the bill owing to my own bad fact-checking.

reader, asked to read more than a hundred manuscripts and pick four or five to send to the final judge. I think the experience will be fun, and it is— for the first twenty manuscripts or so. After that, I learn that it's incredibly boring to read manuscript after manuscript of "I"s asserting themselves and their claims to truth. Listen to what happened to me, they say. They interpose themselves between the reader and the world so everything is filtered through their shadows, so each I stands between us and actual experience. They suppose their "I"s are solid, inviolable, made up of evidence and verifiable memory, that their stories are theirs and theirs alone, and do not think what it means to make a story their own. The more I think about "I," the more self-conscious I get about its proliferation in my own documents, in my emails (in which embarrassingly many—or all—paragraphs begin with I, as if each email is an exercise in assertion, in letting everyone else in on my solipsism), my letters, notes about my experience, these essays, and the way I process it all through I, through these eyes, assumptions of truth or at least verisimilitude.

Each member of the jury receives a small notepad and a pencil to take notes, even though the court recorder is transcribing everything in great detail. We will have access to the court recorder's transcription in the jury room, but it will not become part of the public record. Nor will our notes, I find out.[10]

Looking at MAJ, I feel selfish writing notes to myself on the official jury notepads for what I am convinced will become an essay, though I don't know where it's going. I have already envisioned trying to write something about this experience. The notepads are here for us to be good jurors, to document this case in order to determine whether MAJ is guilty or not guilty, and I am using them to write down facts for later fact-checking; in the middle of the experience I have already committed to processing it for later. This is the familiar economics of writing nonfiction, I note to myself, already a couple of levels removed from what should be my primary task. Later, while we're waiting in the jury room, one of the jurors asks me what I keep writing on the notepads. I tell him I'm taking notes for an essay on this experience, whatever that is turning out to be. He laughs, maybe thinks I'm joking, says, well, you're the writer. The pads are small, too, and

---

[10] They collect and shred the notebooks, so I smuggle mine out in my pants, expecting I will need it for fact-checking later.

the pencils suck, which does not really encourage much actual note taking or writing of any depth. The physical process of it is altogether unwieldy, in addition to the ethical dilemma, since there are actual stakes here. How often is something actually at stake in essays, in memoirs, in most of the nonfiction I read (and perhaps write), I wonder? How often is there actual risk involved, invoked?

I feel is part of the problem, with that I asserting itself in nonfiction, though we can't fault it, lonely pronoun, stand-in for one consciousness.[†] We can, however, fault the assumption that individual experience—sans connection to something larger, beauty or social action, for instance—is in itself interesting as a primary subject. We can fault the I—or at least the text—for not being aware of its own instability. Asserting the primacy of I suggests that we should care about it because it is an I, because it has incurred slights at the hands of others, of the world. And we should care. Sure, I agree with that: everyone is special, deserving of attention and examination. And inhabiting their experience allows us to share it, know it. (This is called *collective knowing.*) But I still don't want to read what most people have to say about themselves if it's just to tell their story. I want it to be art, meaning that I want it transformed, juxtaposed, collaged—worked on like metal sculpture, each sentence hammered, gleaming, honed. For me, the sentence is where it's at—the way the story's told—not simply the story behind the language. The action of telling is fine: kudos for you and your confession, your therapy, your bravery in releasing your story to the public. But telling is *performing,* even if it seems effortless. And writing that story and selling it to a publisher make it product, packaged and edited and marketed. With years of reflection on that story and how it can be shaped as prose (and how its shape changes from our shaping it, reflecting on it), given audience and agents and editors, rhetoric and workshop and rewriting for maximum emotional punch—given the endless possibilities of the sentence on the page, I expect to see a little fucking craft. I guess I want awareness, a sense that the writer has reckoned with the self, the material, as well as what it means to reveal it, and how secrets are revealed, how stories are told, that it's not just being simply told. In short, it must make something of itself.

Of course some lives—many even, and most, if not all—are interesting when looked at closely enough, and preferably with an angle of refraction or reflection. But the memoirified superreal liveblogging culture in which we live has suggested to us—readers made writers, we are all potential content creators, even if we no longer have the time or inclination to actually read—that we should ourselves, unmodulated, automatically matter to strangers.

I wish I cared more about others' stories, and I do, individually (I care about yours, reader, for instance; I'd love to talk one-on-one over a beer), but when taken en masse, in print, read in the hundreds of manuscripts that start with the letter and word I and end up being primarily interested in exploring self without craft or infusion or interruption by the world outside the I—that accumulation of vast and tangible facts, that ball of everything, indeterminate pronouns, that litany of "A"s: billions on billions on billions of individual entities—well, it gets boring pretty fast.

All of this is our fault, writers, readers, publishers, probably, and teachers of writing especially. It is our job to encourage our nonfiction students—those rising, almost completely erect, uppercase "I"s—to consider themselves worthy of respect, of examination. That is, after all, what the essay is all about: thinking, examination, and, at least implicitly, the thing that is doing the examining, meaning the self, the whirring, humming projection of the brain. Because our students often lack much actual life experience (no Melvilles or Hemingways, they), it's easy to focus on what life experiences they do have. Sure, it's partly generational, all those trophies on mantels for tenth place in the track meet or for being the fifth-best student in their graduating class. They are special. They are the future. We teach them well and let them lead the way. They are individuals, citizens: eligible for personal essays or jury duty like any of us, able to sit in judgment of another and to weigh the sorts of proof offered by prosecution and defense. We believe, maybe, in that idea of liberal education, in the importance of individual and increasingly diverse stories, so that we assemble a legion of students and create thousands of writers all working on their personal essays, their family excavations, their memoir projects, most of which are (in spite of what we'd imagine) strikingly similar: they iterate and investigate traumatic occurrences in their or their families' lives and assemble these into variably coherent and complicated, aware narratives.

Well, that's what we get when we democratized literature, when we got interested in all different sorts of protagonists, not just prophets and princes, when we agreed, in the words of Yeats, that "fair needs foul," that "nothing can be sole or whole / That has not been rent."[11] We want the fair, the foul. And we get the fair, the foul, the ghoulish story, the redemption. And all of this resides, or can be found, or can be made up, in the hollows of the I.

As an aside: I do all of this too. I can't see a way to stop it, either, thinking about the I, examining myself (I must face the fact that I do, in the end, find myself interesting, which is good, I suppose) in text and thought. Perhaps the answer to the writing and the teaching and the learning is in *research*, in listening, in exploring, in taking notes. It's harder, yes. It's finding, creating, or uncovering another subject—something else to rely on and parse beyond the self. People know this, obviously, but I don't think we as a caste of MFAs, future serial memoirists or whatever, and those who mock those with MFAs—none of us is thinking about it seriously enough. We don't realize how many of us are doing approximately the same thing. (On the upside, though, those working against this grain may have their work immediately stand out.)

Very occasionally these individual stories are so striking, conscious, and/or artful that they create a heightened interest: they compel us, they cast that spell over our nighttime hours. One manuscript (of the ten[12] I passed on to the final judge of said book[†] prize) recounted her (brutal, brutal) story of incest survival, in which she was molested by seemingly every member of her immediate (and maybe extended—my memory fails me here) family. If true (and if not, this is a perfect exploitation of the flaw in thinking about this sort of nonfiction—it doesn't allow for any sort of doubt; it asks to be taken at face value, as absolute, or nothing), there is sufficient weight (or, well, mass, technically, and when combined with gravity—risk, the power of a potentially killing, attractive force—only then it equals weight) in the story to compel the reader's attention.

Plus there's no time for me to fact-check these manuscripts, or even do five minutes of Googling to see if their claims are borne out, if it's even

---

[11] "Crazy Jane Talks with the Bishop."

[12] I didn't feel like I could send just five, as instructed. Five out of a hundred plus seemed insane. Ten, I thought, left a little more room for subjectivity. And given the similarity of so many of these manuscripts, I tried to account for a number of different stories, shapes. Yes, it was fairly hard to find ten I was actively excited about. But I understood my role as judge was to read carefully, to choose the ones I liked the best, and to send them on to the final judge, not to reject them all as unsuitable, not to be snarky about it.

possible to check. The power inherent in many of them is that they are telling the truth, that it is their story, not how they tell it. It is an attractive stance. The power of confession, of appearing to tell the truth, to initiate the reader in secret, is heady, definitely. It's useful to manipulate in poems, in fiction, and in nonfiction. It creates intimacy, particularly if we as readers feel like we can—we must—enter into belief. We don't get to *choose* to suspend our disbelief, like we do in fiction. Which is why some of us feel betrayed when memoir turns out to be not entirely true. A question I start to ask to ferret out lesser manuscripts is: If this doesn't turn out to be true, do I still care? Meaning: Is it interesting beyond its apparent truth content? Do I still care when the I turns out to be a ghost, when the power of truth slips out of it?

But most manuscripts, while momentarily lovely, fail that test for me. They finally prove to be minor, one-dimensional, in one way or another: recountings of divorce, family strife, death, varieties of sexual encounters, childhood traumas that extend to adult life, references to Montaigne, resonances everywhere, epiphanies coming about once a chapter or so like white noise. They aren't usually all that elegant. These writers presume— and have doubtlessly been told, perhaps in workshops, perhaps by me—that their stories, finally, matter in themselves. Still, I see something in these also-rans: they might be made to matter if explored further, with style, an angle, some kind of action working as a countermeasure against the desire of the I to confess, to tell its stupid story.

Fiction writer Cris Mazza (perhaps best known for coining the term *chick lit* before it was annexed and repurposed by the publishing conglomerates, mapped to slim legs, short skirts, pink heels, and martini glasses) guest edited a special "no first-person" issue of the literary magazine *Other Voices* in 2006. It included only stories told in something other than first person, running counter to what she identifies and rails against in her editor's note as an increasing trend toward defaulting to the first-person point of view in contemporary fiction:

> I am not a fan of the current popular status of the first-person narrator. This is not saying that I am not a fan of the first-person technique, but just not a fan of its current popularity. Think back to when an overwhelming percentage of new fiction was written in the minimalist style. To say, "not every story is best served by being

minimalist," would not be a claim that there are not some very superb minimalist novels and stories. What it would be saying is that when a technique becomes a popular fashion, becomes overused, its special qualities, complexities, and beauties are going to fall away, and all that's left is the faddish use of its most obvious characteristics. . . . [S]uccessful uses of first-person POV underscore the pitfalls of its excessive popularity . . . too many times the use of first person has nothing to do with what the book is about.

I don't object to the use of I (how could I?), but to its simple, unexamined use, particularly in nonfiction where we don't assume the I is a character, inherently unstable, self-serving, possibly unreliable. I object to our unthinking cultural embrace of the I phenomenon, to our readerly desire for unmediated "I"s, for confession booths, for more reality in everything we see, including our fiction. That our cultural interest in the nonfiction I, in individual testimony, has spilled over into the way we approach the short story and the novel, and our assumptions about what fiction is and why it matters. That we are now writing and reading self-absorbed fictional characters without realizing it. And what's worse, that we don't seem to understand (and thus use) this: that our stories borrow the self-importance of memoir (which is at least buttressed by actual, fact-checkable reality), that they fail to consider form, and that they don't do what they need to do as fiction: to tell a compelling story, but also to examine that compelling story and the act of storytelling through the prose, to let the sentences get some traction and complexity, to generate friction against what is being told.

The unreliability, the misrememberings, the act of telling in starts and stops, the fuckups, the pockmarked surface of the I: that's where all the good stuff is, the fair and foul, that which is rent, that which is whole, that which engages the whole reader. Let us linger there, not rush past it.

In the end I sent the ten I liked the best on to the final judge, my duty discharged.

I am thinking about all of this when we are called into the courtroom, and the defense officially, anticlimactically rests, having called no witnesses—not even asking the defendant to tell his side of the story. Thank God this is a diversion from both the I in this essay and the ostensible subject of the essay, or the frame narrative, which is certainly the deliberation of the guilt or innocence of our real subject, the actual dude MAJ sitting forty feet away from us. I need these diversions to get away from this essay being about me. We are not here for entertainment, but to sit in judgment of an actual person. There is something real at stake. If the incest survival story is not finally 100 percent verifiable, and we are let down by it, then we wasted time, maybe a little money, some emotional currency, and found our way to a bogus catharsis or two.[13] At least, we hope, it was a good story. If the witnesses on the stand in this space are not to be trusted, then we could erroneously put MAJ away for years or decades. MAJ sits there and does not look at us in our raised rows on the right side of the courtroom, which I am thankful for.

In his closing statement, defense attorney Miller looks at us and talks about story and credibility, attacks the witnesses' slightly conflicting testimonies, and suggests that there just might be a conspiracy of the (white) victims to accuse the (black) defendant (though he doesn't go so far as to make this explicitly a race issue) and defraud the bank of the approximately $600 by claiming not to have deposited the checks themselves. We can't trust them, he says, on the small stuff, and if we can't trust them, then how we can convict MAJ? And since MAJ put his own real Social Security number on the endorsed checks, not seemingly trying to hide anything, doesn't it make more sense that the witnesses paid him for some service and just won't own up to it on the stand?

The story doesn't have a lot of support, especially since the defendant has not spoken—asserted his voice, his consciousness, his story, that I—during this entire trial. This is for obvious reasons, since he was recently released from prison (we learn this over the defense's objection), and would probably do more to incriminate himself or prejudice the jury if he took the stand. But we are left with no real story aside from the prosecution's version, which is

---

[13] Though the whole point of catharsis is that it is bogus: a construction, that it is an emotional or psychological experience in the audience, achieved via the quality of a performance. So maybe we shouldn't complain if we achieve catharsis at all (though this risks sounding like the physical response of orgasm is the thing to be achieved). We have had the response, and there it is. Who cares if it's *because* we sidestepped our usual reluctance to believe because of the *non* in nonfiction (James Frey) or the near-*non* implied in the allegedly autobiographical fiction of J. T. LeRoy? Who cares if we now require so much reality that we cannot simply give ourselves over to fiction without wanting to parse the gravitas of the author as part of the text?

simply that he apparently is that stupid (in addition to being a recidivist, itinerant criminal), that the witnesses have no reason to lie, and that the documents we've seen tell such a thoroughly convincing story that MAJ doesn't need to tell his. And story here is important. We want to be able to make sense of the evidence. That's how we process information, in terms of story.

Prosecutor Killiman responds to the defense by relating a story of her own. Last week she'd been sure—absolutely, totally, and completely—that she had left her glasses at a restaurant, and after significantly, desperately looking into it, found she'd left the glasses in her office. "We all have memories that are not perfect," she says. She asks us to decide for ourselves how reliable these witnesses are.

Mr. Miller reiterates that MAJ's behavior doesn't show that he was trying to *hide anything*. How dumb do we think MAJ is? we're asked. He says the prosecution's story—these facts, these small holes in the witnesses' testimonies—"just don't add up," and this means that the burden of proof rests with the prosecution. It has not met its burden, so we must find him not guilty.

The court clerk selects (semirandomly—one person has asked to be excused because she has small children to care for) the two alternates, and they are thanked and asked to leave before the final deliberation. I was sure I would be one of them: it would be the most appropriate cosmic response to my attempts to write about all of this. But I am not.

The rest of us adjourn to the jury room and take a break. When we return we must elect a foreperson, who turns out to be me. This pleases me more than it should. I am sure everyone can tell that I am happy with my role, and I am embarrassed that my desire is this obvious. Since it falls to me to moderate the discussion (I have done this before, I think, albeit not with these stakes), we take a quick anonymous vote on paper, and it comes back 11-1, guilty. We discuss, and though several of us are silent, there is no real counterargument. We talk about MAJ's lack of testimony and credibility, the unlikelihood of the story Mr. Miller is telling us. Eight witnesses testified for the prosecution: they told their stories. The defendant did not tell his. We as a jury, as Americans, hold that against him: he had the right to speak for himself but did not. It is as if there is no story without the I, MAJ, on the stand, participating. So MAJ refuses to make himself a writer, a confessor, refusing us access to his story, his experience. And we jurors, as readers, remain unsatisfied. We want access, backstage passes, scoop, an unauthorized biography. And we are not getting it with MAJ. Nor are we getting it in this essay, since I can't stand in for MAJ and tell his story. Or, I refuse to: I could, after all, assume it, connect some dots, make some fiction out of it, please some readers, and make this more dramatic.

But readers are part of the problem. We want drama and we want access to everyone's story. Maybe it's because we are not inclined to trust the stories told by the government, or the media, or business, or each other. Maybe it's because we read them increasingly (as we should) as *stories*. Maybe because we don't feel like individuals anymore, our lives defined by constellations of books and music and preferred hair products, our marketing profiles, as specified on social networks like Facebook. Maybe because of all this we want to assert ourselves, the importance of "us," the importance of "I," and so we demand more I, and more dramatic I, and when the I turns out to be aware of what we demand, what we are watching and waiting for—when that I starts fudging details, confabulating events, expanding time spent in jail, claiming gang affiliations and street cred or Jewishness or Holocaust experience, all to increase drama, sell books, or get TV time and movie adaptations, all to satisfy us and give us what we have repeatedly demonstrated we want—we get angry, and we are angry at that I, and the publishers who propagated and propped up the I, but we should also be angry at ourselves.

I suspect one person either voted not guilty on instinct and stood down in the face of argument, or else simply wanted to put the matter to discussion, which is worthy, certainly, and so we take another vote, and I read the votes off: *guilty, guilty, guilty, guilty, guilty, guilty, guilty, guilty, guilty, guilty, guilty,* and finally, dramatically, *guilty.* We have concluded that we the jury (not we as individuals—who might not want to be held personally responsible) find MAJ guilty on two counts of uttering and publishing. The decision has taken less than an hour. I press the red button on the wall that summons the court clerk.

We file back in, and as foreperson I am asked whether we have a verdict. I say yes. The judge tells me to read the verdict. I am surprisingly nervous here. I read the verdict. The defense asks to poll the jury individually, and we each have to affirm that we voted guilty, just to make sure we can be held accountable—that there are no dissenting Is in we. And it is done. We are ceremonially thanked, sent back to the jury room, and the judge comes in to thank us personally. A middle-aged man on the jury asks me for a copy of the story when I'm done with it. I take down his contact information.[14] We file out and leave our jury badges behind.

The jowly defense attorney stops me on the way out and asks me if there was a single thing that tipped the jury to *guilty*? I wonder if he's asking me as a writer, a professor, a juror, the foreperson, a human, a reader. I say no, not really, but that for me it came down to not having a plausible story from the defendant, but that obviously MAJ couldn't take the stand since he'd only prejudice the jury. He says yes, there wasn't much to be done. His face is flushed. He confesses this was his first case. He asks me if I thought he did okay. I tell him that I had no idea this was his first,[15] and that he did a good job, considering what he had to work with, for whatever my reassurance is worth. I tell him that he was *Law & Order*–worthy. I think this is a compliment.

Half an hour earlier, back in the jury room, I try to convince everyone that they should watch the 1957 film *Twelve Angry Men* (directed by Sidney Lumet). I tell them that all the action takes place in the jury room, like this one we are sitting in, and that George C. Scott is in it, and some other people who are eminent, surely. I trail off, not remembering exactly. (George C. Scott is not in the movie, I find out on rewatching it, though there is a George C. Scott–like character who butts heads with the jury's lone truth seeker, played in the original by Henry Fonda. In 1997 George C. Scott appeared in the for-TV remake, so I haven't fabricated this completely, which is good.) What I do remember of the plot (correctly, it turns out) is this: the foreman asks for an anonymous vote. He collects the scraps of paper and reads them aloud, one after another. The vote is eleven guilty, one not guilty. (I must admit that when this happened in our jury, a part of me was thrilled: the "plot" of our story was prefigured by the plot of the film.) The film makes a compelling argument against reliance on memory, demonstrating how several witnesses in the trial (*Rashomon*-style) have made assumptions, and are unintentionally

---

[14] I've since sent him a copy of the finished piece. I have not heard back from him rebutting or corroborating my story.

[15] This is a minor fiction: at least in retrospect I could tell; his nervous tics, his halting closing, all of this seemed to suggest the fact. During the trial, the judge made a big show of talking about how much respect he had for both the prosecution and defense attorneys, and how long he had worked with them both. Maybe this was an attempt to help compensate, or level the apparent playing field. In the end it appears this story was a tactic, not a truth.

fabricating what they said—they have convinced themselves that what they said is what they remember, that it is the truth, and when they say it, it is inscribed in memory: it becomes part of their psychology—and shows how easily swayed we can be by our own biases (racism is a strong presence in the 1957 film with all white men on the jury). I tell them they should really watch it. (No one on the jury has seen either version.)

I realize that I am relying here on a film, a fiction, to support my point, but it is increasingly likely that what we remember—all of it—is fiction, variously true or edited. It is constantly being reedited to fit our version of events with what we think of ourselves, the narratives we use to define our lives and give context to action, and we might as well admit it.

According to a 2007 article, "This Is Your Life (and How You Tell It)," from the *New York Times*, "Researchers have found that the human brain has a natural affinity for narrative construction. People tend to remember facts more accurately if they encounter them in a story rather than in a list, studies find; and they rate legal arguments as more convincing when built into narrative tales rather than on legal precedent." The article goes on to detail some of the varieties of personal narrative, and how they fit into the larger culture (themes of redemption, good memories spoiled by dark details and disappointment, "American cultural narratives, of emancipation or atonement, of Horatio Alger advancement, of epiphany and second chances"). Legal research—or at least common sense—must certainly bear that out. And of course the more you think about it the more it makes sense: of course we reevaluate events and seeming facts in our lives (or perhaps, in extreme cases, confabulate them) in light of our current mood and psychology, and in terms of how they connect to other larger stories that we have constructed.

I have worked the story of the jury, the story of the story of the jury *(Twelve Angry Men)*, the confusion over my mother's cause of death, my sort-of-screed against nonfiction, and my misdirected and unnecessary colonoscopy (and the resulting insurance story) into the civic service of probing the truth. I have thought about my criminal history as a sort of interesting speed bump in my life, partly because I was not actually jailed, but also because I went on to what I call better things: college degree, marriage, graduate degrees, good teaching jobs, publications. That is a note of redemption I—or you—might be hoping for. So I have reconstructed this story out of other stories, fitting them together so they feel (hopefully) satisfying. And the self-consciousness, the self-analysis, that I return to as a kind of habit is perhaps an antidote to the pressure I feel of writing nonfiction, of claiming that humans can ever actually present the truth, the whole truth, and nothing but, on paper, permanently. That I can realistically trust my own memories when bits of them simply never took. It's embarrassing, really. My story has a little epiphany, too, about memory, which is convenient. And others have a different relationship with their memory than I do, I imagine: hard-core drug users, routine binge drinkers, and those with biological or psychological problems, for instance, all of whom are at a huge disadvantage: they cannot rely on their memories at all. These people who live less-straightforward lives know all of this already, and might take notes, or rely on photographs, or transcripts, or others' recollections, the police blotter, circumstantial or eyewitness evidence, stories they tell or write themselves: anything that can help to bring it back to them, or help them to reconstruct the self.

Amnesiacs with damaged hippocampi (the location of much memory activity in the brain) cannot imagine the future at all, because they cannot frame it in terms of the past. The rest of us can do both: create future out of past experience, and re-create the past to fit the present, and tell ourselves it is true, that we are sure of it, that this we most certainly and definitely believe.

In the end, whatever else this is all about, Michael Antwone Jordan—the dude, the actual physical person in the defendant's chair, not just MAJ, not just a literary construction—is in the center of the swirl of it. I am left with the image of him forced to stand for the jury's verdict. This is a fact. It has to be. It happened. I have the documents. The defendant, having risen, having offered us not one word, not one story, this entire trial, faces us. Or: I have no idea if he faces us; I am not looking at him when I deliver the verdict. I don't remember. I am too nervous. If I think about it long enough, I don't know what the verdict, what the essay, what the self, is about, really. My job in this moment is simply to speak, an *I* standing in for *we*. So I do. And I don't remember what happens next. Nor do I remember what he looks like in this moment, what his actual face looks like. Michael is a faceless, voiceless defendant in this story. He is guilty, he is storyless. Or: He is storyless, he is guilty. I can't, and won't, speak and stand in for him. I can only try to make my own burden of proof, and show you a preponderance of evidence, of fact and fiction, on my behalf. I can only stand up and (think about what it means to) speak for myself.

The asterisk—also referred to as star, splat, Kleene star, palm, sextile—was used in a number of ancient genealogical texts to denote a birth, perhaps the image of the world from the infant's perspective as she is born, or perhaps a microcosm of the family tree spreading out from a central point. The dagger[†] denotes a death. I think of the asterisk as an opening, something rushing quickly toward me, or maybe it indicates us going into it. If you look at it this way long enough it will envelop you. You will become in it, in me, as it, this set of spun "I"s standing on the sides of a pentagon (in this version of the asterisk; in other fonts it shows up with six points), as seen from above. In contemporary texts, it's used to suggest a note on the main text. It faces and annotates the other page, those beautiful mouths moving.

ASSEM-BLOIR†: DISCLAIMER

This is, to the best of my ability, a book† of nonfiction. However, this does not mean that someone else might not remember or interpret things differently. Every experience consists of many stories and many points of view. This one happens to be mine.

I'd not planned a memoir, if that's what this is, and never owned a diary or made notes about the passage of the days.†

The attempt is a very modest one. These pieces do not pretend to be more than a retrospective glance at certain aspects of the cultural history of twentieth-century America. They deal, too, with changes in popular tastes and ideals and attitudes rather than with intellectual history in any profound sense.

And if this be true of such external resemblances as pictorial art is employed to produce it is equally true of that unconscious self portraiture that revelation of the inner mind which is contained in a greater or less degree in any collection of published letters. The interest which such works are intended to excite is in the main biographical and their object is not merely to preserve and bring to light a number of writings of intrinsic merit and beauty but still more perhaps to present to the reader a record however imperfect of the personal characteristics both moral and intellectual of the writer.

Our stories about our own lives are a form of fiction, I began to see, and

Dearly beloved, we are gathered here together today for the marriage of a hundred "I"s in tatters into an *assembloir*, or, if you'd rather, an *assembled memoir* collaged from over a hundred memoirs, contemporary and not-so-much. In others we ourselves are summoned up. Our thinking about the "I"s we read about is our thinking about ourselves, our bodies, our minds, our essays, ourselves. In this we are conflated, and we will pay to be conflated. We will queue to be part of a crowd at an event. We will pay to read these other "I"s in books, to discuss them in book groups, on television, at readings, in our bedrooms with our lovers.

become more insistent as we grow older, even as we try to make them come out in some other way.

I'm writing to approach, through words, that empty shape inside me, to creep around it, like a hunter, to work out how to kill it, to know its territory.

The chronology has slipped, before and after often get mixed. I have tried to keep a continuous story and to amplify it as little as possible with hindsight.

I assume I retain certain features of gesture and mood derived from buried lives.

The names and other identifying details of some of the characters in this memoir have been changed, and a few of the stories told to me by my mother[†] have been compressed, keeping the actual spirit of each but avoiding beating a point to death. These and the other stories in this book are told as I remember them; although through the decades some incidental details may have become slippery as wet stones, icy streets and inclining slopes, they have become part of my truth.

The writing of an autobiography is a perfectly defensible activity, but it is also an exercise in egotism of a kind in which I have no desire to indulge. To write of one's life may be excused either by reason of public eminence or of true greatness, and neither of these conditions fits me very neatly. I have, nevertheless, spoken of my own life in the pages of this book because, to achieve my special purpose, I could not avoid doing so. A word now about that purpose and the measure of personal revelation these pages contain.

Probably in the life of everyone there comes a time when he is inclined to go over again the events, great and small, which have made up the incidents of his work and pleasure, and I am tempted to become a garrulous old man, and tell some stories of men and things which have happened in an active life.

Just how far anyone is justified in keeping what he regards as his own private affairs from the public, or in defending himself from attacks, is a mooted [sic] point. If one talks about one's experiences, there is a natural temptation to charge one with traveling the easy road to egotism; if one keeps silence, the inference of wrong-doing is sometimes even more difficult to meet, as it would then be said that there is no valid defence [sic] to be offered.

Each I encountered is a mouth that we are swallowed in. It's okay to be consumed in an-other's brain as long as we can cast it off eventually, a wig, a borrowed coat, a Halloween costume. I have been thinking about the self, about consciousness.[†] About our ways of trying to represent consciousness: first-person narration, stream of consciousness, memoir, compulsive neurotic footnoting and increasing annotations, essay after essay after essay. They are beautiful and necessary. They are problems waiting to be solved. Ac-cording to a 2009 study conducted by Nicole Speer and Jeffrey M. Zacks, when the brain reads a narrative text, it actually simulates what is described, and reruns the simulation as the story situation changes. Reading is not a passive act; we are simulating[†] another. Anyone who reads a lot knows this already. We try on selves,[†] run simulation programs, enter into magic. The act should not be treated lightly.

When I write, I write necessarily about the past, about something which, at least while I am writing, is behind me.

In this book I hope to tell the reader what I am. It is an answer to literally hundreds of requests for information concerning supernormal perception and how it functions. Since I am the agent of this perception, it has been necessary for me to search for the moment of its first incidence.

Writing has not, as I at first supposed, been a remembering of a concluded period in my life, but merely a constant pretense at remembering, in the form of sentences that only lay claim to detachment. Even now I sometimes wake up with a start, as though in response to some inward prodding, and, breathless with horror, feel that I am literally rotting away from second to second. The air in the darkness is so still that, losing their balance, torn from their moorings, the things of my world fly soundlessly about: in another minute they will come crashing down from all directions and smother me. In these tempests of dread, I become magnetic like a decaying animal and, quite otherwise than in undirected pleasure, where all my feelings play together freely, I am attacked by an undirected, objective horror.

Is it possible, I ask myself, that all this can actually have happened to me? Surely I must be dreaming. I'll fill my pipe and rest a while.

If I have erred in this memoir in recording a name or fact, or recollected an incident differently than another participant might have, I hope you will understand. After all, I'm seeing this through the prism of many years, and sometimes the eye (and the brain) can get a little blurry, as if a handful of flour has been tossed in its way. Here, then, is some of what I breathed in, some of what I saw and some of what I heard.

You must know the proper language in order to survive this sort of thing? Is there no end to it? Certainly there are no heroes and no villains, only misinformed people who with the best intentions in the world are messing up other people's lives.

Here, then, is so much of my life as I believe necessary to an understanding of the origin and functioning of supernormal perception. Nothing that I felt to be pertinent to that understanding has been withheld; nothing not to the point willfully revealed. I have presented the truth as I see it.

There are many lessons to draw from this story. One of them is that it can be dangerous as well as sinful to interfere in the lives of others. If we were God, this might be all right. But since none of us is, and since

Can we learn from memoir? Do we learn from other lives? (Do we even learn from our own?) Does reading experience count as experience? And: memoir as a map—in this case a literal map, but a memoir *is* a map, a landscape, a geography, what is seen and measured by the eye.

we know so little about ourselves, to say nothing of others, it is more prudent to adopt a nonjudgmental attitude and, even though we may be sorely tempted to improve matters according to our own dictates, it is wiser and in the long run more humane to let people work things out for themselves, even when you are sure you know better.

I spend and waste time like a millionaire; plenty of capital on deposit, I will never run short. And forget with the same lavishness; no need to save old memory[†] since new memories pile up, an unlimited supply of money in the bank, a bank as big as the world.

Gradually I pieced together a scenario of clandestinity, of false documents and myriad illegalities.

The present memoir not only serves as a guide to this map, but also contains a varied stock of information, collected by the author, Mr. A. L. Hall, relating to the more practical questions associated with the geology, such as water supply, economic products, etc., of which as yet there has been no connected account available.

The area, from which the material for this memoir was gathered, is coterminous with that of the map, which embraces nearly 180 square miles, or, in other words, the environs of the Capital within a radius of approximately 8 miles. . . . Advantage has of course been taken of the information obtained in areas beyond the limits of the map, especially where such information assists—as, for example, in the case of the Hennops River Valley to the east of Irene—in the proper understanding of the geological problems, with which we are immediately concerned.

As soon as I started to write about my own life, I understood that to speak honestly about family and community is to step way out of line, to risk accusations of betrayal, and to shoulder the burden of being the one who blows the whistle on the myths that families and communities create to protect themselves from painful truths.

When I was young, famous men—usually retired generals, Shakespearean actors, or the disillusioned relatives of such people—wrote "their memoirs." I never read them but imagined them to be the boring ramblings of old fogies puffing themselves up.

I will add a word on another topic. No one can be more aware than I am of the egotistic appearance imparted to this Memoir, and to this prefatory chapter, and to this very paragraph, by the circumstance that I write it in the first person, and speak of it as "my father." This appearance must needs

But memoirists are such easy targets for our scorn. A life described as story is an easy target: how neatly everything fits in, how easy it is to cleave to the norm. If we choose to represent our lives as story, it's no surprise that our stories converge, that we all want highs and lows, the reckonings with our pasts and flaws and loves that we are otherwise incapable of in actual life. Maybe we are all the same, we are telling ourselves, no matter how much we try to invent our way out of this, and that's the thing we can't stand to hear or know.

be so offensive, that it would not be deliberately encountered but for what seem to be good reasons. One of these is, that, as a matter of honesty, I wish my readers to remember that I am writing about my own father, that they may therefore make all due allowance. Another is that I wish to remember this myself, that I may therefore exercise due caution. Still another is, that I was obliged to choose between this way of treating and presenting my subject, and that other way which consists in an apparent withdrawal from all personal interest, and which is a little apt to withdraw from the book all interest whatever. We have eminent American works which repeat the capital "I" to the utter exhaustion of the printer's stock; and certainly this is a great fault. We have others which totally avoid the use of the first person singular, by an unwearied, but somewhat wearying, ringing of the changes upon all the phrases and indirections which go round and round this little word, and are always in sight of it, but do not touch it. This seems to me a great fault also; if for nothing else, because it compels the reader to remember that he who is perpetually laboring to avoid speaking of himself, can never, by any possibility, forget himself.

If this memoir is a little patchier and less organized than some of the others, it suits the subject and the circumstances.

I do not like to judge others. I know now that everyone has their secrets. I write mine down. I carry them lightly inside me. They are almost invisible.

Sometimes all we want is respite from traffic and the sound of other voices, to inhabit the white space[†] in the book, to listen to the silences, each space a mystery, descending light from stars.

VANISHING POINT: FORMER CITY†

851 Turner NW, Grand Rapids, Michigan

In the soon and former city we are in cars. The city, at once itself and every city of this size, too small to have a serious investment in trains or subways or elevated trains, is entirely about the car, even more so because of its proximity to the deteriorating factories of Detroit. Long stretches of Turner and Front avenues on the west side run underneath and along the edge of U.S. 131, an unappealing, though not appalling, divided highway. Construction is snarling, barely started, everywhere. This is the Midwest in summer, knot after knot of traffic being rerouted, streets reconstructed or resurfaced or in the process of being completely removed. This is the city: glorious, mostly; in flux, always. How can we relate to it but by car, by bus, by trails of gasoline and refueling stations every mile? This is not critique but celebration. It is grid, speed limit of 25, pylons on their sides adorned with flashing lights, their batteries dying like animals hit by cars and expiring along the edges of the traffic stream. Ahead the Varnum building glistens, buttery and blue. It is 87 degrees and the world is filled with sun as in commercials. Cars pass in the one remaining lane. The architecture here and everywhere is various. Only in the planned suburbs and historical neighborhoods is there an attempt at uniformity. Here are four-square Victorians, bungalows, and ugly sixties ranch-style dwellings that resist description.

Houses for sale line this and every other street in spite of CNN.com's citation of Grand Rapids as one of the ten best real estate markets in the United States for the next two years. They forecast a 2 percent growth. Thrilled, we are all selling our houses. Others are being foreclosed. Still others have abandoned their mortgages for warmer climates, or have lived in the house so long that they have transformed it with equity and want to take advantage of the plunder market.

(This is June 2008. This is just before the full extent of the huge housing collapse becomes known. Still, this place,[†] this city, has not boomed. It will not bust as hard as other cities. In the wake of the collapse, we come to understand the fiction of permanently increasing housing prices and the sexiness of growing American equity.)

Sixty wires—at least—string across the street to houses from telephone poles, electrical boxes, cable boxes. Green scraped-up minivans. What is the character of a city like this or any other? The S-curve curls through downtown dividing (loosely) West from East, following the Grand River out toward Lake Michigan where the rain will eventually end up.

*

Blocks south the highway divides and off-ramps into Interstate 196, which will take us toward Chicago. The graffitied supports for the elevated highway have been recently recovered by murals depicting stylized scenes of rapids. They are beautiful. This is soon to be our former city and this is a new discovery. The nature of cities—or other places—is that they evolve and bubble up discoveries on closer examination, especially right before we leave them.

*

38 Front St. SW, Grand Rapids, Michigan

Further south a white minivan sneaks by to park in front of what appears to be an abandoned warehouse with "38 Front" spray painted on the corner. Two men go in with a box of food, what looks like sandwiches and drinks from Jimmy Johns. The building must contain more than space.[†]

One of them looks at us as we look at them. They raise their sunglasses to see better and put them back down. The lot is abandoned. This warehouse overlooks another abandoned warehouse with new cars parked in front of it. More inexplicable graffiti has occurred here and is beautiful even as it connotes, what, gang culture, something to be feared? In the four-story building there could be anything, windows broken out by the barrel of a rifle trained on us or cars crossing the river on the interstate. Another warehouse is being built up just down the block in the midst of these other repurposed buildings. Each has its old purpose—manufacturing, probably, or processing or distribution, one of the logistical ends of cities with their economies of scale and distribution. Words painted on the sides of buildings have almost been erased. One reads "[unreadable] Grand Rapids." It is obscured, painted over or faded. No faces appear in the taped-up, cracked windows on the third floor. Anything could happen here. Anything could have happened here. It is all potential. Potential is mystery. A thousand thousand processes underpin the operation of the city. The electrical towers and generators are everywhere, surrounded by what appear to be heaps of dirt and scrap and compost, abutting huge pipes and NO TRESPASSING signs. We don't know very many things.

*

On Godfrey St. SW we are increasingly desiring to know everything about the city, to capture its incomprehensibility, its complexity, to reduce it, to keep it, to saturate it with queries. Sad that this is a reaction to leaving it, to becoming a former resident, a post-denizen. We pass Curve St. and the Macinerny Wire Co. sign, Advanced Fulfillment Inc. with its ambiguous raison d'être. We had not seen or traversed this section of the city before. There is always another city inside the city.

*

The city contains countless stories—known and not, fiction, fact. This makes it crux, concentric circles of, center after center, layer after layer.

In our office in the house in the city it is silent by the city's standards.

Birdchatter, airsong, motion of bikers. We do not belong to the city or it to us.

*

How is it that only when we are leaving the place we become voracious for it, that because of the limited time of the engagement it is now more precious? It is a limited edition, a single run, and soon it will be gone. Or we will be gone from it. Like the last slice of pizza, though we are not hungry, we want it inside us, to be consumed, as knowledge, the last chapter of the book[†] before sleep, the last half glass of wine in the bottle or sip of spit-flecked beer in the 40. Completion, maybe, is what we're after, a full set, or achieving the end of something (a video game, a monster of a novel, a narrative, a race).

*

The night is another city entirely. Grand Rapids is deluged with rain, four inches or more in downtown in the last eight hours, the streetlights extinguished, some power out throughout the streets. Thus there is silence, running water moving toward the sewers, not the usual at all. We drive around taking photographs at night only to find ourselves objects of suspicion. Cop cars trail. Because of Homeland Security there is doubt about photographing public places. Only a few children shriek. The cars continue to move past, but no one is returning from the bar on foot tonight. No kids pissing on our front yards or the side of our car, no too-loud conversations from oblivious couples or singles on Bluetooth cell phones with earpieces shaped like commas as they puncate their sentences with laughter or other sounds. Right now just the sound of the city settling and emerging from weather, the question mark tails of cats just up the street, distant sirens portending doom or false alarm.

Even the domicile is beginning to look less like itself. Its faults are plain, its walls bare, items stacked in boxes, the space in which we have lived beginning to be unlived, that transformation to another tenant just a week away. If we could hear the contrails of planes at street level they would hum exhausted everywhere. It would be beautiful enough.

It is not one of the first cities, the New Yorks, Chicagos, Los Angeleses.

It is not even Detroit, that former city slouching from and returning to the past, but the second-largest city in Michigan, as we say and have heard quite often. It gets shit on as a former city quite a bit, in Michigan, state in a state of depression, and Grand Rapids as a leftover, in the southwest corner, warmed-over, not much to offer. This makes it a runt, beloved. And the silence and the darkness make it beloved, each of the houses on the street retracted into its own compartment, any life it might have within pulled back into its nighttime shell. So it is alien. There are no fireworks, even. It could be a film of the city instead of the city itself, or the city covered with a thin film of silence, sexiness, mystery, city but a zero, latent, waiting.

∗

Downtown we enter the other city, the city of businessmen and pay-for-parking in lots and decks, of public transportation and buildings exceeding the Victorian three stories of the city.

Underneath this city is the story of fluoridation, the story of artist Alexander Calder (the first NEA-funded public art project was his), the story of furniture boom and bust, and Amway gone Alticor gone Quixtar. The story of traces left behind by people who have come to and erased themselves from the place. Our students email us a mounted photo left behind by one of the former tenants of the building. The student and her roommates have been pilfering the collected left-behind items by former tenants, collected by the landlord, and stashed in the basement. The building builds its trace. We can sort and sift through it as if ash or a thin layer of dust (which is mostly human skin) collecting over everything. As far as we can tell we left a box of our prized LPs in the basement of the former building in the former city, the Stickley Mansion, built by Gustav Stickley's[1] brother. We think too often about these remains. These will be a find for someone, especially now that vinyl has made its way back toward the collections of teenagers who buy music, probably in opposition to the sterility of electronic, downloaded songs. Someone will sort through those, our former landlord or another lord of the land.

After leaving the city, we rent a condo, which is barely a space at all. Included in the kitchen cabinets of our new condo we find: one metal

---

[1] Arts and Crafts movement furniture designer.

colander, a couple of plastic Tupperware containers, a champagne flute, and a glass vase with plastic flowers. We archive them above the fridge in the most remote cabinet. Next to them is the cat dish bequeathed to us by Patricia Clark, whose cat, Jack, had died, so it just reminds us of that, unfortunately. We returned the couple of kitchen chairs to our friend Emma after she moved to the former city, after she had given them to us in the former former city, and we had her schoolroom clock, which we loved until the cord broke and shocked us well enough to pay attention. Most of our things are either hand-me-downs or found at garage sales, thrift stores, etc. They have histories. Some are our mothers', and remind us of them. Many of their things have been saved by our stepmothers, who compensate for being stepmothers by summoning our mothers' memory[†] as if from sleep or glossy dream. These items constitute a life, a habitat, an intersection of a lot of different lines.

Underneath this city is all our histories, where our self-described redneck neighbor lived, where our third-grade teacher, dead now from cancer, grew up, where we lived during that one whiteout of a year before we broke up with our partners and returned to the living nightlife fray. Where we used to eat breakfast before the waiters there pissed us off and we were forced to find another greasy spoon. Where we first kissed our lovers, or caught sight of them through the lit-up window as we drove by and nearly wrecked our cars, but it was worth it, just to have that memory in our frozen brains.

Underneath the former city are the remains of a dozen former cities, surely, ethnic groups driven or wiped away by force or trickery or natural disaster. Everything is underneathness; everything is history, snowfall accumulating after snowfall, except never to be burned away in spring. Instead it is contained—to be transcended or plundered later for information, setting, maybe, memory, configuration of ley lines somehow amounting to what can only be a partial representation. It ebbs and it ebbs, and so do we, and soon it too will be gone.

Sites like Wikimapia, a website[†] wiki devoted to annotating a global map, or the viget.org Grand Rapids wikiproject, try to collect ever more user-entered data and information, to document these places, to populate them. This is a collective human endeavor, filling space with information, with stories, theories, forecasts, histories of the place. Collectively we are writing the world.

THE ESSAY VANISHES

I have wanted to vanish for a very long time. Even now I feel myself dissolving under the pharmaceutical haze of one Benadryl that I take to aid sleep. I don't do this every night—usually it's a half tab, not a whole; I am wary of the body's ability to adjust to pills. It used to knock me out. I would take one, and in twenty minutes I was gone.

In the Midwest your best bet for disappearing is a blizzard, a confluence of weather that erases human trace: footprints, animal tracks, ski marks, tire tracks, even directionality, horizon, sense of where home might be or from where you have come. We have space† for disppearing into under whiteness—acres on acres of trees and field beyond field. Rainstorm can't quite compare. It lacks the flattening, whiteout quality of snow blizzarding everywhere, which erases depth, which covers everything, reduces it to an impenetrable, shaken globe. Perhaps the dust storms of the desert or the plains can compare but I don't remember them, or never knew them at all.

One way to be erased by a blizzard is to die in one. It's easy to get confused in the midst of swirl and lose your bearings. Sometimes you lose your clothes. One strange but not uncommon feature of death as a result of hypothermia is the phenomenon of paradoxical undressing, where you get confused as you get colder, and start to feel overly hot, to shed clothes, strip and expose the skin, which accelerates exposure and death.

The result is that you find bodies—often enough the bodies of women—stripped and frozen, and police assume (usually erroneously) that a sexual assault played a role. They quickly enter fiction, if not myth, those murdered, assaulted girls. It's an easy enough leap to make for those unfamiliar with death by exposure. Theories for the cause of paradoxical undressing include the baffling of the hypothalamus, the part of the brain that regulates body temperature. But either way we strip and disappear. We grow warm and then too cold. The snow erases us again, maybe not to be found until spring. Weather rubs us away. Our bodies are stripped for the coroner and disappeared when the ground is warm enough to dig the hole in order to erase us from the surface into the body of the earth.

*

Is any of this—

*

The vanishing desire is what leads me to periodic alcoholic obliteration, self-effacement. The removal of the conscious mind from the process. The removal of inhibition, gate left and down out of the pasture. The removal of the body from the process. Who hasn't thought of attending his own funeral with the maudlin organ and the eulogies and seeing everyone else who's sad to see you gone, looking down at your reconstructed face at the visitation. You would show the world, you think, what you meant to them, by your disappearance.

Words do disappear. They are erased from hard drives, recycled in boxes strewn about the campus, thrown away and composted, letters in landfill, stored between the pages of library books forgotten about and returned, deposited in drop boxes for processing in the future. Essays find their way to light in literary magazines or other magazines and are forgotten, if they are read at all, returning to the backlists, the periodical indices, the library databases too expensive for most libraries to carry. Those words posted to the Internet remain if service providers archive them, if they continue to provide a service. Or they stay hard-drive encoded or magnetic on disks. I buy old computers from Salvation Army and Goodwill and St. Vincent de Paul and try to plug them in, bring the files, whatever personal trace they hold, back to life, and print them out or save them onto my own magnetic storage device. And when the data is gone, the mercury remains as metal footprint somewhere in the earth. We think of our words as permanent but they degrade by degrees in air, as if echo, as if they remain compressed rings of energized air reverberating down canyons forever, forever.

This is beautiful and reassuring, that they don't much matter, finally, that they are data in the wash, that they are consumed or that they recede into memory.[†] So every impression we make—electronic or physical with pencil and the bruise left by that pencil on the hand over instances of revision—has a half-life of its own. Perhaps the half-life, the half of the life, is that half that occurs when it's remembered, retrieved, found, iterated, or indexed, and the remainder of its life consists of erosion, corruption, or revision until it lacks definition, is no longer recognizable by anything or anyone.

This should be helpful for writers of nonfiction in particular. No matter how much you think your essay/memoir matters it does not, not really, not likely, anyhow. A fraction of 1 percent of essays might finally matter, be remembered, have some effect. This is a fraction worth aspiring to, but it is an asymptote, that graph line indicating the unattainable, increasingly approachable but not reachable. Your friends, your family, if written about, no matter what you have eventually to say—all of that will be washed away. It is temporary, this effect. It lasts only as long as memory can persist in consciousness.[†] The most we can ask for is latency, for a word, a fragment, an idea to pop back up in thinking (*Bar-Bar-Bar*, say the barbarians, according to my British Lit I professor from years ago, and that's why they're called *barbarians*, and this bit is still live in my brain, and I get an email these years later nearly in this moment of composition that he has just died), or conversation, a kind of shared magic, the sudden access to a memory stored in fat and synapse underneath or shot through some other useful bit of information that has now receded in its place.[†]

*

Haven't you had the pleasure of finding scraps of paper tucked in textbooks or novels bought secondhand and wondering at their meaning, if they have meaning anymore, if meaning can be transitive, reinforced by years?

YOUR PERSONALITY

Name _Mrs. Jenetta Woodward_

Address _____

1. Center of attention
2. Full of ideas (good)
3. High aspirations
4. Magnetic
5. Amiable
6. Impressive
7. Resourceful
8. Subtly demanding
9. Quietly efficient
10. Shrewd and discreet
11. Friendly
12. Charm
13. Inwardly disturbed
14. Easily contented
15. Hard to satisfy
16. Honest to a fault
17. Unselfish and undemanding
18. Suave
19. Vivacious
20. Social ease
21. Inarticulate
22. Hospitable
23. Domineering
24. Reserved

YOUR MIND AND ABILITIES

1. Active mind
2. Adaptable
3. Aggressive
4. Artistic
5. Brilliant
6. Cautious
7. Concentration poor
8. Cultured tastes
9. Decisive
10. Deliberate
11. Direct
12. Dislike of detail
13. Exaggeration
14. Reasonable _(heart)_
15. Gifted
16. Good judgement
17. Imaginative
18. Inconsistent
19. Intuitiveness _(some)_
20. Inventive
21. Keen
22. Level-headed
23. Literary
24. Logical
25. Love of variety
26. Mathematical
27. Observant
28. Precise
29. Open-minded
30. Perfectionist
31. Quick
32. Forceful
33. Ruled by mind _(heart)_
34. Skeptic
35. Set opinions
36. Uncertainty
37. Unpretentious
38. Versatile

Hi! Sorry I've been so long in answering your letter - but I've been awfully busy both at work + on my time off. I'm trying to get organized so I can go on vacation April 29 to May 16 - Would you be going to Clara again sometime? Perhaps we will see you soon to chat? If you are here! Hope you enjoy yourselves...

_Yours truly & sincerely,
E. Coleman_

The facts: Mrs. Jenetta Woodward has scrawled this note in the margins along with a self-assessment of her mind, abilities, and personality: a permanent decision, even if the author, the referent, has been lost. Or perhaps this is the work of the person who finishes the note on the left and not Mrs. Woodward at all. The handwriting seems off from the name line to the signature line on the note, and the name changes. I am no graphologist nor do I believe in graphology as a way of telling us much about the contents of the human personality, mind, abilities, or natural tendencies. But I do like -ologies of most sorts, the desire to taxonomize and analyze any realm of human endeavor. The best part is, of course, that she has modified the "test," changing "Intuitive" to "some Intuitiveness" and "Ruled by mind" to "Ruled by heart," a very different proposition. This is one of the better found documents I have discovered in the books I buy secondhand, and it presents us with puzzles. Who is L. Cochrane, and is the name spelled that way? Who is Mrs. Woodward? What is the relationship of the personality test to the letter, and these two to the text, or each other? Who writes a letter on a personality test? Or who once did? And how did this document get discarded here? Mystery awaits. The results, these characters, these plotlines, have surely, nearly disappeared.

A quick Google search reveals only one result for "Jenetta Woodward," being: Jenetta Woodward, 25, Domestic, Tennessee, Female, from the Liberty Twp., Barry Co., MO, 1860 Federal Census at the Eagle Bottom Post Office. It's doubtful she is the preparer or original receiver of this document, but still it's an interesting result. Jenetta Woodward, it would appear, does not rate more than one hit on Google, which means in this contemporary way she does not exist. Perhaps the name is concocted, or the document is doctored. Or she lacks notoriety or public presence enough to be in the present tense anywhere on the web. And that I recedes back into the wash.

*

"Inclusionism and deletionism are opposing philosophies held by editors of Wikipedia, a popular online encyclopedia, regarding the criteria for including or deleting content.

"On Wikipedia, deletionists generally argue for the deletion of articles that are short and poorly written, unreferenced or referenced only by

Web-based sources and blogs, that appear to fail the community standards of notability, or that exclusively contain trivia or popular culture references, as well as of [sic] other types of articles deemed unencyclopedic.

"Inclusionists call for retaining more content, for higher tolerance of 'stub' articles, and an acceptance of notable blogs and other Web-based sources."

These quotes are from the Wikipedia article on deletionists and inclusionists, a binary whose positions could be applied to nearly any form of information or collection. Are you an inclusionist or a deletionist, the future personality test might ask you, I mean, philosophically, thinking broadly, like think harder, dude? Do you reflexively cut things out or stitch them on? Protect the tower or tear it down? Iron patches on your jeans or shotgun blast them up? Which is the better modus operandi? Would you rather have the world slowly, asymptotically approach One or Zero?[1]

*

Bodies—or parts of bodies—approach zero. They vanish along with the names for them. The appendix has outlived its usefulness, we think— though this week science returns it to the fore, reminding us that "the abundance of circumstantial evidence makes a strong case for the role of the appendix as a place where the good bacteria can live safe and undisturbed until they are needed," and that thing we had thought obscured continues to persist. The appendix, it appears, is a safe haven, an inclusionist. The physical memory of my mother's[†] body has gone from me, though those that I have physically loved, in college, for instance, still remain as memory, as fantasy, as something to return to unbidden at night before I dissolve, attenuate—

*

---

[1] Think about this in terms of the proliferation of memoirs. You no longer have to be notable in order to write a memoir and have it read (though that helps). We are all useful, worthy of examination. We are all notable. I wouldn't argue that any individual person is not notable enough for Wikipedia, which, unlike a print publication, might have a nearly unlimited number of pages. Nor would I argue that memoirist X is not worthy of a memoir. Worthiness can be assessed later; after all, the magic is in the telling, in the transformation of life to art.

Vanishing makes for excellent headlines. Tidal pools, glaciers, teenagers, endangered species, oil reserves, lakes, beachfront property, college girls: Everything is going, leaving us, raptured or consumed or kidnapped.

I once believed I could vanish and be gone—only a zero left behind. *Local man disappears inexplicably in a furious burst of smoke*, the headlines would read. Or *man dies of overdose*, if that's newsworthy enough. If I were to commit suicide, I have always thought I would blow myself up in an Upper Peninsula Walmart. Achieve notoriety, if not notability. Have my disappearance noticed, noted in obituaries, or left to persist as mystery, which would be better. But what if I were gone and there was no trace no wake no bread crumb trail no unfinished manuscripts with sentences ending in ellipses . . .

*

DETECTIVES investigating the disappearance of Vicky Hamilton yesterday announced they are now conducting a murder inquiry, 15 years after she went missing.[2]

BLOOMFIELD, Conn. — A man charged in the disappearance of a teenage girl who was discovered hidden in his house Wednesday filed a sexual abuse complaint on her behalf before she vanished in 2006, police said Thursday.[3]

FIGUERA, Portugal—Three years ago a happy-go-lucky girl, who loved to chat with everyone she passed in the village, went missing and has never been found.[4]

Telegraph newsdesk: A MURDER trial jury has heard how a teenager

---

[2] "Police Launch Inquiry Fifteen Years After Girl Vanished," Michael Howie, the *Scotsman*, November 16, 2006

[3] "Police: Suspect, New-found Teen May Have Had Ties," CNN.com, June 7, 2007

[4] "Figuera—Tragic Tale of Murdered Girl," Alison Chung, *Sky News*, February 27, 2008

literally vanished without trace when she disappeared three and a half years ago.[5]

*

The essay perishes. It perforates, is perforated by bullet holes.

As the body perishes so does the essay, which is like a body. I would love to see it worn away—shot, maybe, with a shotgun on a target range. Can you bring your own targets to the target range? I want books destroyed by time, eroded by weather action or Scrubbing Bubbles.

I desire leaves and wire and spinning. The fan is on and in the window, gateway to the wider world. There appears to be nothing beyond it. Autumn, maybe, hypnopompic, hypnagogic, always on the edge of something that makes less sense than this.

Summer dissolves into colder times. And then the reverse. It is flux.

Fanhum. Airmotion all around. A cooling system, an insulation against that outside.

Tiny flies move against the screen of the laptop, thinking it paper, a place to land, a beacon. Or maybe they think *light,* which means to them mother, or infinity, or God, or whatever. I wave my hand, and they are gone as if in a blizzard. Then they return, a wave, departure, diaspora. Repeat.

*

Is it gone already? The litany of stupid things you said to those you thought you loved, or maybe did, before you didn't? You must have made inconceivable promises, unsupportable by facts, in your ardor, and that counted for something, and were you asked to hold to them, or were you not? And the repository of the asinine acts and phrases you repeated, the nightly iteration of your humiliations before sleep, are those gone, too, so you can dissolve and release the brain to do its unconscious thing?

*

---

[5] "Murder Trial Hears of Covert Surveillance of Suspect," *Blackburn Citizen,* June 11, 2007

Fall away, amnesiac. I can barely remember important information from last year, what I cared about, what that matrix of brain was thinking then, what prompted whatever actions.

Those girls are disappearing. I read about it on the news all the time. Faces framed by blonde hair, by dark hair, by red hair. They barely are more than faces. Sometimes they are interchangeable, those girls, one mistaken for the other, one dead in a car crash, the other in the hospital for weeks before their real identities emerged and the news facts had to be changed, the right funeral performed, gravestone changed, one girl brought back to life, the other disappeared into the ground.

(The faces of my former students, saved to my hard drive for this very reason, disappear. I remember fewer, even from last semester. I remember girls the best, unsurprisingly, tending toward sexual preference or away from the legion of baseball-hatted dudes with clotted hair. They still sometimes show up in dreams, disturbingly, a year later, or longer.)

*

Underneath his carefully manicured lawn? Cut up how? No, I can't—

*

Found:

Chas. Olin is a large-headed baby in a huge white frock. She? He? Wax mannequin? Stunned or bemused god? Whatever, it looks deranged. But wait—that whatever isn't fair. Behind the disambiguation, the mystery, under the frock, is a she or a he, one of two probable futures, and certainly one real person (unless we're going mannequin). It's easy shorthand to wonder. But no, Chas. is Charles Olin, the photographer who gets the byline, not the baby, and that's his studio in Cassopolis. It should be so obvious. But it's obscured until I push past the first scrim of apparent meaning.

The child is a triangle, nearly, the pyramid of proper eating or of rising action, from the trick of the perspective partly as well as the glory of the frock, long enough to stand in for a bridal gown. The curl of hair on the upper left is mine, or possibly a cat's, caught accidentally by the scanner and digitally fused to the photograph. I could Photoshop it out, but I like my trace added to this other trace, a pair of ghosts, meeting of like minds, unnamed baby and I, large-headed both. The baby's all, like, where am I, nameless, sexless, propped up on some antique bench in the recorded past for your posterity, and you should count my tiny fingers or give me a frickin' cookie or give me the dignity of a name before I disappear again.

*

Found documents bring pleasure. They are textual, factual, corporeal. Their age and randomness sex them up, make them physical, erotic. As surprises, they please. It is easy to fetishize the found. Unlike digital information they are scrawled, etched, annotated, the product of handwriting, that skill we were graded on every year in school and that still shames me. I got a D in handwriting from Mrs. Drenowski in fourth grade. My parents retain the scrap that proves this. My name is surely buried in their records, or the school records, along with my studently deficiencies.

*

(found marginalia—not mine—from a copy of Woolf's *To the Lighthouse*):

—Not easy for her 2 concentrate
—she lives in a textured, material reality

—incapable of imagining an abstract table —> its [*sic*] a particular table (specific)
—Ramsey can describe any table
—she understands people
—trying to understand life
—comment on women
—wants her husband 2 feel important
—social organism
—everything premeditated
—think about Wordsworth and his attitude toward nature (Tintern A. forms of beauty)
—lighthouse=reality/life
—once I was innocent, look what I am now

*

More embarrassing are the notes I've scrawled in margins myself, typically in books I read for one class or another. I cringe on seeing them, encountering this evidence of a former self. It is as if the mind on display (crudely, crudely) is an old shell and inside it is the current mind. Or my metaphor is backward: the old shell is smaller and the new one must contain the old (or did the old evolve into the new and discard its elder self?). I am not sure. This is one good reason to discard the books, to drop them at Salvation Army or Goodwill and inflict those thoughts, those inflections, on another.

I run across some notes in my handwriting (opposite page) that detail, apparently, plot ideas for a cyberpunk novel. The handwriting embarrasses, the thinking embarrasses. Reading it is a form of self-anthropology. The yellow legal pad embarrasses. The red pen, too (so dramatic!). But it's my embarrassment. It's still recognizable. It's still my mind, my body, posed for posterity. It's paradoxical: nakedness comes tied to disappearance, prefigures it. It could be the dress rehearsal. When the body has been stripped down to just the body there's not much left to take off or disappear, except years from the mind, except "Sleaze/Shadow."

It is partly a reading history: I recognize obvious traces of William Gibson, with the added bonus[†] of Descartes. What's really weird is that looking at

Subjectual
Objective
truth

ss data   lock-n trace

~~lops~~ band   voltage jack

s a   graphical user interface — networks

rates   ghost in the machine

                 AI

                 clipping leads — remote uplink

                 René Descartes

                 new modem type with digital fiber optics

S, CIA, FBI)   lockin, GUI again

cel and   persecution by some unnamed (gov't) agency

ine to   over AI research

efng   expert systems

tly lock   auto-hacker

.   maybe hired assassins

                 Interrupt Lock, computer burn

                 ⟶ trace + burn

ckground   Virus

s) ank   Trojan Horse

                 Logic Bomb

                 Sleaze/Shadow

                 KC12.0

sional   Descartes Project — Ghost in the machine

a small   — AI / Expert System

ents to cyberspace "rooms."

it, sure, it's me, a younger iteration. The D-grade handwriting, the fetishiz-
ing of the technology, the dramatic gestures. But I don't know or care to
know this person at all now. I have shed that self, or think I have. Mainly
that former I remains inside, shellacked over or overgrown by tree rings
or scar tissue. Maybe in time it will become beautiful like what oysters do
with grit, or like how the saguaro cactus handles a foreign object. I now
know what more of these words mean (an expert system, for instance). I
wish I had left this in someone else's book[†] for them to find and puzzle over
instead. I'll leave it here for you without further annotation.

*

SOME OF THE GONE:

Alison Arseneault
Andrea Haven—murdered
Angela Joesbury—murdered
Anne Wolsey
Brenda Wolfe—murdered
Catherine Gonzalez
Catherine Knight
Cindy Beck
Cindy Feliks—murdered
Dawn Crey—murdered
Deborah Lynn Jones—murdered
Diana Melnick—murdered
Dianne Rock—murdered
Dorothy Spence
Elaine Allenbach
Frances Young
Georgina Papin—murdered
Heather Bottomley—murdered
Heather Chinnock—murdered
Helen Hallmark—murdered
Inga Hall—murdered
Ingrid Soet

Jacqueline Murdock
Jacquilene McDonell—murdered
Janet Henry
Jennifer Furminger—murdered
Jodi Watts—murdered
Julie Young
Kathleen Wattley
Kathryn Nankervis—murdered
Kerri Koski—murdered
Laura Mah
Leigh Miner
Linda Grant
Marcella Creison
Maria Laliberte
Marnie Frey—murdered
Michelle Gurney
Mona Wilson—murdered
Olivia Williams
Patricia Johnson—murdered
Rebecca Guno
Richard Little [a man's name, obviously, oddly, haunting our list]
Ruby Hardy
Sarah deVries—murdered
Sereena Abotsway—murdered
Sheila Egan
Sherry Irving—murdered
Sherry Rail
Sheryl Donahue
Stephanie Lane
Tanya Emery—recovered
Tanya Holyk—murdered
Teresa Triff
Teressa Williams—murdered
Tiffany Drew—murdered
Wendy Allen
Wendy Crawford—murdered

Yvonne Abigosis
Yvonne Boen—murdered

This list is copied and pasted from somewhere online. The link is gone. It is not in my browser history, not on my bookmarks, not on my delicio.us shared bookmarks, not archived on my machine. It is no longer documentable. Does it still remain true? Perhaps I printed it out, committed it to the older technology of paper. A website[†] memorializing those who have disappeared, as I remember. Girls. Vanishing girls. Killed-off girls. There is something about a girl. Girl is vulnerable. Girl is acted upon. Girl is something else. They vanish in hotels, in borrowed spaces, in electronic spaces, like the virtual online chat rooms that you hear about in periodic news reports.

Found (below): Post-it in California.

Best-case scenario: I presume this had been attached to a computer, a hard drive, all the data erased in accordance with some policy. There are other theories. Data fragments remain unless overwritten. They'll find your secrets and your pornography unless you're careful, unless you encrypt it, unless it appears to be meaningless strings of text and numbers scrambled and rescrambled. We are thankful for deletion, for erasure, here. We ask to be forgotten, to have our voices and fascinations disconnected from our identities, our bodies.

*

The lady vanishes. The body vanishes. Air trace around the bodies vanishes.

*

Have you ever slid a car into a lake? On an inclined plane, a boat ramp maybe, leading down to lapping water, put the thing in neutral, engine off, or maybe left it on and let it sputter as it extinguished, but more likely not, in a secluded place, among a thousand pines, just pushed the car in and let the sound and fact of water take it over? If you leave the windows open it goes down much faster.

*

No, I've never—

*

I don't mean to suggest that these girls disappear for us, that our fascination with them makes us audience and entertained, makes us track them down or watch the story unfold on television, makes us responsible. If we called out less at their disappearance, though, I wonder if they would vanish as often.

*

All these found documents are related. Each of them is attached to, evidence of, some remaining charm left behind, one of the missing girls, real, honorary, or imagined.

*

My friend's father is found in the dawn light, or so I visualize it, the air cool and the water barely moving, having hung himself (apparently) from a watertower. The body exists there—in police record and in memory, or in imagination. There is no explanation for his death, but when I see mutual friends we speculate; we want to know. We want to squeeze event for meaning, so we can resolve the dissonance, the mystery, and file it safely away to be repurposed for later bar or other narrative. But the why is not on the scene, or not at hand, or too sordid to be released (this last one is my theory), so we feel, we fill that void with theory. His end, tragic as it may have been, is a question mark, a starting point, an opening.

*

We see the emanation, a little light beyond that gap, and want to walk in through it. We want to walk, to sleep or perchance to dream, our way to meaning, to the other half of interrogation. There are thousands of boat ramps dotting the state of Michigan, overlooking its 11,037 lakes (according to the DNR). Countless cars, and if one vanishes, who would think to look for years of rusting and wheeling downstream, being submerged in silt, in reeds, in darting fish or unseen currents? It is almost a beautiful idea.

You're in the wilder portions of Michigan or any other place; you are hiking, maybe, or wandering down some unmarked trail. You happen on an abandoned mine, or two abandoned, rusted cars now home for skunks, or maybe on the remains of one of so many sunken wrecks while diving in Lake Superior. Something perished here, you know. Something was abandoned here. This is how I envision our future: surely we will be erased by cataclysm, self-made or other, and our ruins will remain.

*

Tucson houses one of several airplane boneyards in the United States where planes are retired from active duty and more or less mothballed. It is beautiful, of course, all this collected war ruin, and like most ruins it immediately suggests the transitory nature of all our sophisticated technology. Officially called "The 309th Aerospace Maintenance and Regeneration Group," it has over 4,000 retired aircraft. They do not sell directly to the public, though you can buy some scrapped items through sellers such as Boneyard2U, which maintains an eBay store. If you're into memorabilia or vintage technology, you may buy instrument panels, landing gear doors, "T33 throttle quadrants," flight manuals, aircraft engine pistons, aircraft ejection seats, automatic pilot modules, vintage radios, and a commercial airliner ashtray and a "TWA flight attendant evacuation panel" from a civilian plane.

These skeletons are everywhere.

*

Or maybe self is a wiki: anyone or anything can change it, but we could trace each edit back if we wanted to. The wiki retains its history even if it is no longer visible. Not palimpsest exactly, but maybe more a book, still bound, but each page opaque, consecutive. If we want to risk it we can turn the pages back, cycle through each edit, and watch the brain grow stranger and more distant from the present. We cannot fully erase a thing except via chemical or psychological intervention. Or erosion.

*

Sleep is a disappearance, too, a disruption. We are in the car. I have this dream sometimes, or rather, it is a ritual, one of several I deploy to summon sleep. I think of the lake, the water warm, the sun tucked away behind clouds. I am in the car. The mind is in the car. It is approaching water, and then it is out in it, everything streaming through the vents and the seats and the cracks and everything. It could be terrifying, but in this instance it is not. I approach the water level, or it approaches me.

*

And when the name has its explanation, when it has been attributed one meaning or another, a cause, a motivation, when the court motions have been made and the bodies populating the seats in court and facing the television after dark in this state and in a thousand others—what then? The name begins to mean less and less. Sure it stands in for something, a blackness, a gap, a poster against domestic violence, or the name of a child on a law, but the woman, the lady in the lake, the girl begins to bleach herself out in our memory. She starts to disappear. There are a lot of names. Countless, almost, and all girls, all these voices in the margins, in the documents stuttered throughout a collection of books, my own motivational litter. I want to remember them, to iterate their stories. I want to comb through them all, to come through them into knowledge, if not understanding, to black text on a white page by way of answer. Each becomes a bracket. A bracelet. A brackish image moving, blooming under water, over and over. Sleep is starting to come to me. The vinyl seat is cold. The water unnatural and warm, a womb, a bomb, an asterisk, already spreading.

*

And what of you, you who are already forgetting?

*

And what if this, the text, forgets its referent, its birth mother,[†] the point in the main text from which it descends? Must it proceed and asterisk out, a shooting star descending through the atmosphere, from nothing, sui generis? Or it might rise up from each dust mote, each discarded thing, your shredded recyclables on the curb, your collection of miniature fantasy figurines that have not been touched since childhood, but that you keep as a reminder of who you were. It proceeds from spittle on a harmonica, slivers of lyrics to a hymn, what your brother said when you were eight, the information you committed to diskettes a decade ago because you thought it then important. Now it is simply magnetic trace, corrupted, barely readable. But still there is life there, even if in data fragments. All human lives can be described by this esoterica, this collection of descended asterisks. It's only in the tiny that anything matters or exists at all.

VANISHING POINT: PANERA

In the Panera Bread Company in a suburb of Columbus, Ohio, just outside our hotel room, which is to say almost nowhere, we sit at our laptops watching others at their laptops, watching us periodically, wondering if we are perverts, or what is up with us. We are in a city.[†] We are in the Midwest. A girl in baggy shorts watches a film with headphones. Surely we think perverted thoughts. A man with a tiny, seemingly homemade laptop pecks away at the flat keyboard in front of him. The room is centered around a display of delicious, almost-plastic-seeming bread, and a gas fireplace that emits, for the time being, no heat. For the last several months we have been playing a video game called, overdramatically, overlong, *Shin Megami Tensei: Persona 3 FES*. The idea of place[†] in this particular game is an odd one. As a recent transfer into a high school you have the option of exploring one of six locations, depending on the day of the week and the time of day. It's not atypical for video games to limit your interactions with created places, quite often pretty but generic, where you can find Character X to whom you must give Item Y in order to advance one of several plots. Usually as the game progresses the available list of spaces will increase as a reward and incentive. We want to crawl every dungeon,[†] open up every bonus[†] area to our prying joysticked or keypadded eyes. Playing video games is already a weird inversion of space.[†] We explore virtual, created spaces represented on our monitors or television screens. We

63

play first-person or third-person (there's one conceptual game that lets you play second-person, and surely it must be disorienting), maneuvering the camera and the onscreen character that we control to watch ourselves move through space. Sometimes these spaces light up, indicating we have explored them, or they stay dark, indicating the unknown. Panera, like any other chain, is a known quantity. We come here for breakfast because we like their pseudoquiches and their coffee is reliable, but most important they always offer wireless Internet for free. So we can come to any Panera and plug in to access the electronic space that has almost no connection to our physical space. True, signals and data from far-off places can take a little longer to reach us, something you notice when you try to download software from a South American mirror site, for instance, but effectively we are equidistant from almost all electronic spaces. Perhaps *spaces* is not the right word.

In the game you can take on different personas in something called "The Dark Hour," an hour that occurs every night at midnight, but occurs out of time: most of humanity cannot experience this space. Your character is one of a small team of high school kids who have the ability to summon these personas, each of which has its own avatar, its own strengths and weaknesses, and can be deployed to destroy a variety of potential enemies. The act of summoning the persona is accomplished by pointing what appears to be a gun at one's head, suicide-style, and pulling the trigger. There is a burst of light from this simulated suicide, and out of the head emerges Slime, Ares, Alp, or Nekomata, which can be combined to create new personas that are ever more powerful. It's a strange game and at moments quite terrifying. You are exploring some dungeon again with your team or alone. These other others come out of you and battle, then return, and the Dark Hour is over, and you have to negotiate the social world of the high school, clubs and classes, and ask girls out on dates. It is compelling. We are compelled. We want to play it more.

In Panera, the earbuds in so we are partly in our inner space. The classical pumped out by Panera is interacting with *The Orb's Adventures Beyond the Ultraworld* (expanded two CD UK edition). We see these two laptopped people and they can see us. We are here and we are not. We are together on this page, in this line, moving down the text block. We are in my head. It is no accident. It is fall. Fall is beautiful in these midwestern spaces. It is evidence of time passing. In Arizona the sun is nearly constant: it seems content with this. There is no changing of the leaves. There is no opportunity for reinvention brought on by the feeling of fall and the seasons changing, the new school year, the new football season. The Panera is in a subdivision North[†] of Columbus bounded by highways without access to foot traffic. Trying to find a space to run in is frustrating since it is not built or meant for foot traffic. You cannot get here by foot. We are not sure there is much of a here to get to, by car or otherwise. Everything is *there*, not here, a conflation of the two, everything is always elsewhere here. The buildings are half-empty in the surrounding area, one chain-sounding restaurant after the other with doors closed permanently, darkened windows. We ran by them. We thought seriously about breaking in to explore those prohibited spaces. We even tried the doors. No luck. Panera is doing fine with its faux-Italian illustrations on the walls. The Buffalo Wild Wings is doing fine. Columbus appears to be doing fine. The oddly phallic Winking Lizard tavern is doing fine. We will probably eat some sort of wrap there in a couple of hours.

Here in this midwestern space one is aware of flatness and humility. Nothing is meant to awe, except maybe the football stadium. Panera is filled with artificial,[†] nameless things, these semicomfortable chairs, the lights from boxes. The bakery equipment that our brothers tell us is so cheap to install that Paneras are the most cost-effective franchises to open up in America. The coffee that comes in the exact same "Featured Blend," "Cafe Blend," "Flavored Blend," and "Decaf" as every other Panera we have ever visited. It is surely reassuring. It holds us in its arms. The caffeine is all around us and our heads begin to float a little. Nothing outside any of the windows gives me any sense of scale or being anywhere. There are no landmarks. There is hardly land. It is comfortable. It is beautiful. The staff meanders around the place since they are contemplating closing. They will lift us up and sweep us out with their brooms and outstretched arms and voices and return to their other lives, perhaps at the BP gas station (with its fancy new green-looking logo) where two nights ago we bought the same beer we often buy in other places. We think we saw one of them there at 1 am, also looking for beer. She bought cigarettes too. She looked exhausted. The light was fluorescent and we had flown in an hour before. We were there, we are sure, but where is that there now? This place is fluid, replaceable. Fragrant. We are protected. We are barely aware of being anywhere.

My resistance to memoir is multifold, is many, is plethora. Even as my gut reaction is fascination, an admiration, almost, at the (good) memoirists' ability to divine and analyze and discuss publicly their own lives. I admire this in my students' work, when they angle inward and really lay themselves bare in prose, or seem to at least. (*Seem to* is all: I doubt mightily the human capability of really laying ourselves bare, of putting aside all the thousand onionskin wrappings of psychology and defense, the feints and apparent confessions and everything, keeping us from really getting to the center of anything.) And the memoirist, or the personal essayist, the confessional poet, even, or the autobiographical writer—all of these aspire to this impression of true candor and openness. So I admire this capability in others even as I fear[†] it in those I have loved, if they were to lay me bare, or lay themselves and their relationships with me bare, not even to get into the psychological horror of getting the memoir treatment from my family or my wife. I'm also unable or unwilling to take that task on. Where do you go from there? Isn't it a feint anyhow, a screen, a scrim of the apparent? Of course it is. These texts are crafted (or they should be crafted) and facade behind facade presented for the reader's pleasure, or the reader's horror, or the reader's wide-eyed gobbling-up of information. But there is always the reader's experience, though the text should not cop to thinking of it, and, so doing, break the spell.

EXTERIORITY

A PIECE BEGINS, A SPACE[†] BEGINS WITH THE TITLE AND THE BYLINE AT THE TOP. THE HEADER ANNOUNCES ITSELF AS A PIECE OF WRITING WITH ITS OWN AUTHORITY ON THE PAGE. A PAGE IS AN ACT, AN ART, AN ENCLOSED SPACE, A BOX, A ROOM. I WANT TO FILL IT OR FILLET IT TO COMPLETE IT OR TO TEAR IT UP AND GET BEHIND IT: THESE ARE THE TWO PROPER RE-SPONSES TO OPEN SPACE. TO FILL, EACH LINE I WRITE MUST STRETCH AND FLUSH FROM LEFT TO RIGHT. IT MUST FORM A BRIDGE, A BRACKET, STRIPE, A STRATUM, A STRAFING, FROM HAND TO HAND, FROM THE EDGE OF ARTIFICIAL[†] SPACE TO THE EDGE OF ARTIFICIAL SPACE. THE END OF THE PAGE TO ITS OTHER END. EACH MARGIN IS AN ARBITRARY LIMITATION MADE FOR HANDS, FOR HOLDING. THERE IS NO MARGIN HERE, WHICH MEANS NO SPACE FOR YOUR HANDS TO GO WHEN READING IT, TO ENABLE PAGES TURNING, TO ENABLE THE CONVE-NIENT BURNING OF THE THING IF THAT IS WHAT MUST BE DONE WITH IT AFTER IT IS READ. WHICH IS SUGGESTED. TO READ THE PAGE YOU MUST COVER IT OR FIND A WAY TO PROP IT UP. CHARACTERS ABUT THE EDGE, THEY LIMN IT, ARE OBSCURED BY IT. THEY RISK BEING TRIMMED, ACCIDENTALLY RENDERING THE TEXT LESS READABLE. AT LEAST ONE HOPES OUR CHARACTERS ARE AWARE OF THE DANGER THEY ARE IN. THIS IS NOT A STORY OF SUSPENSE

648 CRESCENT STREET NE, GRAND RAPIDS, MICHIGAN

It is so hot that I have resorted to sitting in the bedroom with the air conditioner set to 65 and blowsy. I have felt some pity for my cats and have left the door propped open enough so that they can get in, in theory, but not so much that I will lose all of the good air to the outside world. I like the outside world a lot, like it to ravish me with its temp-tations, the variety of things I love that come to me through it: good beer, disc golf, aromatic coffees, Playstation games, strong books. My wife is out **67** of town—a rarity, since usually I am the one who travels—and I am here

in the house, this space, without embrace, alone. Huge explosions from
68   fireworks dominate the nighttime shockingly often in summer in this
particular city† and maybe in every city in the world, each a replica of
this, I think: you could almost stack them up, one atop the other, or overlay them as if they
were all printed on transparencies, and see what sort of inkblot sort of thing, what epiglot-
tis, what Rorschach glottal stop is formed by their shapes. Things explode here more often
because Indiana is close and many things purposed to explode are legal there, or because
this is a city and we live downtown, centered, nearly, in the zip code, and almost centered
in the city, really, which is in the center of the suburban wreath fanning out from here
I am close to the center of the house, actually, though not by design, and the air conditioner has drowned out much of the exterior sound, which is about all I have at night by way
of proof that the exterior world still surrounds me with its vast and open sparkling arms

Very rarely am I given to silence, and I am not sure what this means (that unsurety a silence in itself), whether it be sentences that stretch out like tributaries, or a predilection
for sound, for song, for voice, for filling up the air with energy, others' or my own. I was in
choir, show choir, chamber choir, various shitty choirs in which we embarrassingly sang the
theme from *The Golden Girls* as well as "We Didn't Start the Fire" by Billy Joel, accompanied by a slideshow (depicting events and personages from the song: Ho Chi Minh, Richard
Nixon, the moon shot, Woodstock, Watergate, punk rock, Reagan, Palestine, the Ayatollah
in Iran, Russians in Afghanistan, etc.) that illuminated the darkened auditorium, turned
it into a sort of temporal space, and presumably prompted chuckling. We did not do jazz
hands, however, so I have limits. I played first bassoon in the Riyadh Symphony when I
lived in Saudi, and played in many other bands before, though not as much after. I like explosions, too: those fireworks have often been set off at my hands, though since my friend
blew most of his hand off, that particular diversion has receded from my life. I love the sudden loudness when I am the one starting it, setting it off. The cats are very aware of my
movements in the house because it is loud and it is nearly feeding time, and so they will
soon swarm me or attempt to gain the lap, or perch between my chair and the Playstation
2. It is lame indeed to write about one's pets, but with my wife gone they are here and I
am here and so we circle each other, bodies orbiting something, in the center of the house

The world is in a variety of motion around and above this spot, though it—the spot, our location—is in no way really central to anything unless you count the county, which unfolds
around us, or the surface of the curved world receding in any direction equidistant. Jet contrails are traces overhead, reminders of travel all around and above us. A thousand head-
lights pass and pause and pass again because there is construction on the block just North
of us, so traffic has been rerouted on this residential street. Sound and zoom: the brilliant
sound of the Ford Festiva towing a boat slowly up the twenty-five-degree grade of the hill
that is the street outside my house. Two interstates meet less than five miles away, and pour
themselves together into another major highway that is undergoing significant reconstruction right now, and it seems always, too. We are part of the American project, cars shuttling

constantly around the city, reduced to bits of data, when seen on camera or GPS from afar. Cell phone frequencies are all around us, people expounding to their lovers or whomevers, and radio, too, and satellite television broadcasts, the thousand lines of electricity, and air, and biosphere, the blogosphere, the gases circling everywhere, permeating everything, not to mention people walking shirtless up the street and drinking because we live close enough to bars to make this a regularity.

Part of my week-long project in my wife's absence is to make some major changes in our sole full bath. I have been mostly hard at work attacking a variety of projects that I have never tried to accomplish before, such as removing a wall from the bathroom, pulling out the old tub surround and lath and plaster, replacing a window with a glass block one, removing the sink and replacing it with a new pedestal one that is a reproduction of a $2,000 sink from Restoration Hardware (one of the most fantastically named stores I can imagine, with its implication of our particularly American desire for history, how it apparently once was, having centuries less of it than Europe with its thousand cathedrals and protuberances), and putting down a new layer of linoleum over the last one, which we do not like, no not at all. As soon as I tear into the house, though, I realize it has a history, and it's obvious, sure, that this house is a hundred years old, and was transformed from apartments into a single family dwelling. All the bedroom doors had deadbolts removed before we moved in, leaving zeros, circular spaces in each door that I covered up with metal plates. The door is a door but it is also a hole in the wall with a hole in it stopped up by a metal plate. Zero becomes dot, disc, pie, ceases to signify. When I pulled up the tub surround, I found newspapers stuffed in crevices as insulation. They are hard to read—so brittle that you can't unfold them without their breaking—but at least one lists a date from 1983, which is the year I turned eight (a year after my mother† died, completely decentering the former life).

Others in this neighborhood have lived here all their lives, and when they walk by the house at night and I am on the porch, we converse, and they attest to how it was before they installed the interstate through the center of it, dividing neighor from neighbor. It is mixed racially, economically, socially, and that mix† (and the neighborhood, and the idea of neighborhood, of identity) is one of the things I like about living in this city. The city. It sounds glistening and bustling and new, though it is not all of those things all the time. I have not lived in one, not really one of this size, at least, before. It's large but not gone mega yet. It, like the state, is dwindling slowly. I mostly like it, am pleased by the random lives of those around me, and their trajectories, and plus we get to own the house until we move or die or give it up or burn it down, or abandon it to banks. Everyone in this neighborhood has an old house. We all work on restoring our houses. It is like any other diversion or obsession.

Inside one of the bathroom walls that I tear apart in order to install a backing board for the pedestal sink, I find what seems to me to be a thousand razor blades. A thousand is hard enough to conceptualize so I'm not sure how many there actually are, to be honest. But they reside in a wall cavity and spill out like coins when I open it up to get access to the studs. The plumber I call to come out and advise me in the reconstruction says that I'll have to tear out the wall for them to install the sink, since the pipes need to run up through the wall, and so I do it accompanied by trepidation. At every stage of this project I am anxious: these are things I haven't done before. Even firing up my new miter saw, for instance, seems like it will slow me down; trying to figure out how to assemble it takes on its own complexity that, added onto the combined complexity of these mostly simple projects when taken individually, seems suddenly insurmountable: a huge and tangled skein. I am frozen in these moments, wanting instructions on what to do from someone more senior than myself—my dad comes to mind, whom I assisted on a variety of home improvement projects when I was younger, or the great male mind accessible on the Internet and in books.

When I actually tackle the individual projects: learning how to frame a window properly, for instance, or how to tear plaster from the walls, what a backing board is, and how to install it, then each opens up to me like a secret room in *Super Mario Bros* or in a dungeon[†] dreamed up by a dorky Dungeon Master and explored only in a shared *D&D* fantasy. They are not easy, not exactly, but they are logical, masterable, understandable, like any other sort of knowledge. This is like school, I think. There's walls. Some tools. Some equations. Plenty of punishment if you screw it up. There are books, diagrams, terminology. I can be comfortable here.

So I wonder at those razor blades: *booby trap!* I think, sudden solipsist, or pessimist, protagonist in my own video game, thinking the world—this house—is somehow out to get me, that it has locks to be picked, traps to be disarmed. Or maybe these are the blades of so many discarded daggers used to fight homunculi, wizards' familiars, warlike gnomes, and I have stumbled into a long-abandoned battlefield. On the phone my wife suggests another explanation: the shortsighted razor blade disposal slots that you used to find in bathrooms. For those who salvage vintage bathroom tile and fixtures, caches like this are not an unusual find, but I had not taken apart a house before—I knew it only from its exterior, or from the exterior of its interior, the space we make as rooms, not from inside the walls. Up until now I have known only the living space, that which is inhabited, perceived, not the making space—the effect of structure, not its skeleton. Who cares? Just throw them in the wall for the future.

Everything takes longer than I'd imagine. I will not get all the finishing work done before my wife returns: I will have some drywall to patch, some trim to put up, and the sink and shower to be connected by experts. As it is I will barely have time to get the major things done. And this is without really tearing everything up, stripping out the subfloor and getting at the pipes, pulling out the bathtub and giving the house a colonoscopy. As if I could actually tackle many of these things. Well, I think, I actually could if pressed. This is the epiphany, then, that I am capable. This is a particularly American story, one of hard work and industry eventually approaching mastery, so that is satisfying and familiar and somehow male, and that is good.

At one of the local instances of Home Depot I see a call for people to sub-
mit their stories of home reconstruction or renovation. Everyone has one, **71**
they say, a success story, a narrative of home (meaning self-) improvement.
Anyone can do it. We will show you how. You can attend "clinics" at your local store. (This
week they offer "Tiling Floors and Walls," "Installing a Chair Rail," "Installing Under Cabinet
Lighting," "Installing Faucets and Sinks" and "#20 Race Car"—you know, for kids!) The rise
of places like Home Depot and Lowe's corresponds with a rise in the prevalence of DIY culture, magazines like *Martha Stewart Living,* the eco-hipster-cool *Ready Made,* television shows
like *Pimp My Ride, Flip This House, Miami Ink, Extreme Makeover: Home Edition*, which will
come to film an episode in this city in less than a year, and MTV's gaudy and excellent *Cribs,*
plus whole television networks like HGTV, a rising national obsession with individualiza-
tion, customization, the realization of our alleged dreams, and, most importantly, the realization of our dreams of capability, of being able to do these things ourselves, potentially to
ourselves, and of creating or restoring the illusion of age, history, a vintage. We have history
over here in the states, these media suggest. We make our history. We make it over and over.

I can understand building a house, making a domicile, erecting a building out of nothing but
forest and nails and concrete, and calling it one's own. But the house that we bought was built in
1901 by someone else's hands. It was remodeled poorly in the 1980s, then remodeled again, also
poorly, less than a decade ago. I imagine at least five families have lived here before us. The idea
of bodies passing through (and passing on in) a house like this—our house, we call it, our space,
our proprietary world—is a weird one. I know people who prefer not to live in a place† that has
housed others' bodies, others' body odors, pet danders, histories (hence the love of designing
one's own house, having contractors erect your structure to spec so you are the only one who's
ever lived there: this America is yours and yours alone, you say). It will look like other houses, but
it will be different, because it will be yours. You can arrange the bathrooms where you want. Put
four on the first floor if you want to go crazy. You can constrain your space however you desire.

Our friends Erik and Nicole sold their house in Salt Lake City to move to Grand Rapids. They
made a good bit of money on the house with the then-booming market out west, but they found
out just a month ago that the people who had bought their house—which took no small amount
of remodeling, I am sure, given their collective penchant for dreaming up and doing things
themselves—had torn it down entirely and built a new one in its stead. It must be irksome to have
spent that much time, effort, and money on working your house into a system that you can inhabit and derive comfort and energy from and have it—your labor—torn down so someone else
can make a new house in its stead. On the upside, though, is the notion that the house was yours
last and no one would come in later to make it their own, make it over in their own stupid image.

Outside the city the city gives way to Meijer superstores and Bed Bath & Beyonds and then to
strip malls that dwindle down and terminate in hills and fields fulfilled with corn or other grain.

Beyond this is more of this—field, forest, field, river, road, field, until within a couple of miles of Lake Michigan's edge, at which point beaches and cabins and boat launches and bars begin to take hold again until we founder, end in water. This part of the state makes industry of the outside—tourism, the beach, restaurant patios, boats and glistening varieties of boating accessories, Jet Ski rental, tackle, kites, bait.

Michael Carmichael, of Alexandria, Indiana, is the owner and keeper of the world's largest Ball[†] of Paint. According to the website[†] RoadsideAmerica.com, this is not to be confused with a paint ball, "which is a hollow shell filled with liquid paint," but a "ball of paint: a solid mass of thousands of hardened microscopically-thin layers, methodically applied atop each other." As of 2005, it had almost 19,000 layers and weighed over 1,300 pounds. Carmichael is making a pavilion for it, to keep it safe from the weather, and as a kind of point of pilgrimage for those who, like readers of RoadsideAmerica.com, go out of their way to visit weird and often oversized (and hence mystical or at least puzzling) sites while touring through this country with its lot after lot, its quads, its hectares, its acres, of open space.

You can see cross sections of it online at the website, its fabulous set of concentric almost-rings of succeeding paint layers. It is beautiful and pointless, there somehow only for itself, to serve no purpose but to be coated, to get bigger, maybe to model the ball of a planet that we are on the exterior of. It might aspire to art. Or maybe it's a metaphor. You can visit it, and Michael appears on the Ball's website courtesy of his obsession, and people come by to see it often. You can sign the guestbook and put another layer of paint on it if you visit: it is free to do so, though donations are appreciated. As such there is some tourism money brought into Alexandria, a town with a typically grandiose midwestern name and referent. Its pointlessness, its levels of exteriority, like thousands on thousands of those Russian nesting dolls, requires a sort of archaeological or anthropological approach. What is this thing and why does it exist, we wonder, and so we stop over on our trips crisscrossing America via road, and we can be part of it, we guess. We can have our names involved in it, in the *Guinness Book*:[†] we can be part of history, its accumulating strata, layer on top of layer, simulated geologic forces, pressurized by those above and those below, and that is no small thing.

My approach to the world is all about controlling my environment. I sit in one of many coffee shops in Grand Rapids watching a guy play a mandolin furiously, eyes closed, fingers jerking and tapping back and forth. It is a kind of un-self-conscious magic that annoys me at least a little bit and makes me want to hit him with a rolled-up REM/Losing My Religion poster. I do not do this. It is air-conditioned here. Though I wear headphones, the mandolin and conversations slip through. Humidity is everywhere in this outside world, but I get too sticky too fast, and want inside. I want shelter from weather. A house is key, though we don't have an internal locus of control like central air conditioning. I would dearly like it: I prefer about 65–70 degrees with low humidity, good light, clean air, coffee easily available, perhaps a minion to mist me then dry me as I type. Really what I want is some kind of robotic exoskeleton to keep my exterior exterior even when I am outside, or failing that a magic bubble, a Comfort, 12' Radius spell, like you might get in a too-mellow game of *D&D*. When I was fourteen and I had a paper route delivering copies of the *Daily Mining Gazette* to the houses lining Woodland Road in a town where there were no longer any working mines, I imagined that I had a magic bubble filled with sun slash warmth that would keep my body at the right temperature, unaffected by weather—rain, snow, cold, anger, sadness, death, or whatever.

Everything about a wall asks us to disregard it. The paint, the drywall or plaster and lath, the joints in the wall drywalled over and sanded and drywalled and sanded and primed and primed and then drywalled again because you screwed it up before but only realized your error now, and then sanded and painted and painted: it all asks us to disregard it, consider the wall a negative, a nothing, a curve asymptotically approaching some limit, a surface to adorn. It is the edge that suggests structure, the divider that forms, that allows, the room, which grants us privacy and the portioning out of space. The wall is the end of the room and might as well be the end of the world, growing slowly smaller as you paint each coat—until you tear into it, or until it breaches or shows signs of stress. Then it requires your attention.

It is not something you think about as having contents, substance of its own. You don't think about it, which is the point. It's like the margin of a page. It abuts. It frames. It's hollow; we should hallow it, this insulated space, this vapor barrier against what is outside the interior, what is in the wall, this locked-in, buried, compartment, this closed, this covered zero.

The wall is a stratum too, its repeated layers of paint and wallpaper a minor wonder of house geology, a history, worthy of tracking and tracing. This layer has lead. That layer is in a color that's impossible to find anymore even though Ralph Lauren tries to simulate it. This wallpaper must have been amazing when they put it up, but God, it's hell to get off again. When we cut out drywall, or plaster, and surgery ourselves into the lower reaches, we find something new.

But now we just want it to flatten and dry so we can and will hang our shit on it. The wall is necessary, both as limit, architecture, and shelter, but it's not much fun in itself. In the coffee shop, the bathroom walls are just repainted a brownish color, a thing I barely noticed, and only because of the new paint smell. The paint (new paint, especially) gives illusion of a continuous, singular surface, a background over the real background of the wall, which is the genius of paint. They even painted the molding and the trim so that there is no opportunity to consider one wall apart from the other, except geometrically, or from the ceiling or floor or trim. The overwhelming impression is that you are in a space, a formed thing, but you're not encouraged to think about it as form, as construction, that it is made for you, to keep you in.

Even the finished ceiling in our bathroom, which I hadn't thought about before cutting into it to add in the venting fan, has evidence of patching. Cracks spider across it. They suggest fault and stress. The plaster came down when I cut into it to make the hole for the fan and I have had to patch it up with drywall mud. You can read my work on it if you look closely, though I sanded and sanded and was patient like the instructions said. On the whole I did not do all that great a job with this particular element of the project. You can see the cracks, the tracks of one of my trowels, the marks of the tools used to craft it: and since you see it, the surface is obvious: it is obviously a surface. If we live in this particular space long enough, however, like always, we will eventually forget.

Dust clouds the air outside the window and I lose sense of perspective, scene. Inside again. It might be rain, I think, a mist, or a trick of the eye with its glowing retina trails when closed. It is space outside, and I know this because of sound and depth. Cars approach and move by. ~~I have built this thing~~, I think, the house, which is not correct, so I strike it out but leave it in the essay as a trace. I redid the floors, though I didn't install them. Ripped out the carpet with its thousand animal scents, scraped hundreds of yards of black glue with a scraper and a heat gun, then sanded them down with a rented behemoth of a power sander, losing all sensation in my hands and arms. Applied layer on layer of polyurethane, one of the most wonderful-sounding chemical products that you can buy at Home Depot. It adds surface to surface until the surface becomes more uniform. The floor is bright, shining pine, made smooth. Standing on it you can see outside, but because of the distribution of light if you were outside you could not see in.

I am comfortable in the sleepy hollow chair in my wife's office. It is weeks later, and she is gone to work and I am here alone, sudden solo star in what is usually a binary system. Both of us with animals inhabit the total of the space. The animals are not allowed in several closets or in the bedroom at night. That space is ours by necessity. But she is gone—into the outside world, a mile or two downtown, teaching—and I am here. I could sit at the center of the space, right by the chimney tower, from which point the house has started to sag away. A couple of inches anyhow, I'd guess. You can see the slope in the bathroom with the doors that still are more or less perpendicular, but the floors have sloped away, exposing angular slices of light from the other side.

We could prop the house up if we wanted, slowly jack it up a quarter-inch a week, and rebuild the foundation, trying to restore it to its original condition if we wanted to make it more closely resemble how it looked when it was built. These materials have weakened, compressed very slightly over time. They are of the earth and of the world. If left to its own devices and unmaintained the house would fall apart within a hundred years, return to its components.

The thing that attracts me most to walls is the idea of permanence, of protection, of preservation, of separation from the world. Same with books. We consume and are consumed by them. When we bury our noses in books we might be half-dead to the world outside and all of its pleasures and pressures. As *stanza* is Italian for *room*, we inhabit poems as we inhabit books. And *paragraph* is from the Greek, παραγραφοσ, where a break in meaning occurs and something new begins. Space intervenes. Only by separating like from like can we discern order. Books are exceptionally durable as technologies go. I could sit in this room for years and I would decay before either wall or page would. Even digital devices lose charge, become inoperable, if they don't corrode away entirely. Consider the idea of the *Necronomicon* (from the *Evil Dead* trilogy of films, or the version originated by H. P. Lovecraft, if you like), allegedly printed in blood on human skin, and containing the words of, as Lovecraft has said, "an image of the law of the dead." The body made book. The book not accommodating of the body's needs to read it, margins, etc., but made of body, gathered together around a spine, bound in one kind of flesh or another, our favored leather bindings, the leaves' dried pulp of bush and stump. We use the language of the body for the book. The body of the text. This room is rectangular, like the page, the pine box coffin. It is a container for my speech, for my silence, for the line of nothingness that keeps them apart

Bodies end, and books do, as do rooms and houses, finally contained against whatever is outside them. They are meant to be bound, to constrain a meat against the exteriority of the world, white space, wind action, that would pull it apart. My work on this house is done for now, I think, as I tread its floors, run my hands along its walls like I think my father would proud upon a job's completion. I line the walls in my office with books. Yesterday, I put a few pages of an abandoned book inside the walls as a note to whoever lives here in the future, time capsule–style, before I sealed it up, or at least I tell myself I did. I should have put some Borges there, or Philip K. Dick, or something visionary and meaningful, though more than likely this house—these walls—will be knocked down before anyone opens up the walls again, or it might be reduced by rising water or terrifying wind, tornado on its way to an appropriate trailer park, termite infestation, terrorist action, manifest destiny and the progress of the interstates, apathy of its inhabitants, poor typography, bad mathematics, lack of love, or any of the thousand other enemies of structure, which is all that protects us from white space, blankness, ether, and weather, whatever is outside and after this

The snap of art onto life is bothersome, too, a delinquent, a troubled fit. I would like to say that I resist it more than I actually do. For the most part I don't buy this art as life, which means the art is not executed well enough, because it is all art, this apparent artlessness, birth dates beautifully inscribed on china and kept forever. There's a reason why memoirs tend to be described in the same rapturous, more than slightly breathless terms on the inside flaps, the blurbs, the marketing copy. Sure, it's marketing copy, and marketing begets more marketing, and it's a genre in itself ("a powerful, honest account," "riveting, heartbreaking," "haunting and riveting," "shows us what it means to be human," etc., and really I mean etc. since the list could fill a thousand footnotes like this one), but it also tells us about exactly what we want when we say we want more memoir, more truth in the stuff we're reading: we want to be reminded about ourselves, uplifted and edified through narratives that are really dreams of what we hope our lives could be like. What if my memoir isn't edifying? Isn't uplifting? Doesn't show us something about what it means to be human? It would do better to forget about its overall effect, to focus on the smaller things, actual evidence of actual lives.

ANDER ALERT

In a shameful, shameful paroxysm of self-Googling, which is like looking through the world's trash for iterations of your own name, I find that I have a Wikipedia page (!), and it is on the verge of deletion for "lack of notability." This is the situation. Who among us is truly notable, I wonder, large or good enough for the deletionists? Admittedly, after faking a few bits on Wikipedia to support a bar bet, I edited my own page to increase my age, push me closer to death and withering. People would take me more seriously, understand my hair loss better, my sudden attempts at wisdom. I added a note that "He is a charming douche indeed." Who bothered to read these pages anyway?

Notability, according to Wikipedia guidelines, is based on secondary source coverage of a person: "If a topic has received significant coverage in reliable sources that are independent of the subject, it is presumed to be notable." Unsurprisingly, this is often a very contentious discussion as Wikipedia volunteers argue and debate the ethics and esoterics of what exactly qualifies someone or something as being notable. The conversation itself is remarkable and worth reading: it's worth just looking at a week's list of "articles for deletion" (AfD) and tracing the ongoing conversations as they trail off into meaninglessness and Internet flaming. Being slated for deletion—a fate much worse than having never been included at all—pisses me off. I hope for a champion, someone to come to my electronic wikirescue. None come. Days† pass. So. It falls to me to do some dirty work trying to prove the notability of "Ander Monson." The phrase "Ander Monson" gets 9,700 hits on Google when put in quotation marks to better refer to Ander Monson, though Ander Monson is often enough misreferenced as Anders Monson, Ander Munson, Anders Munsen, or, most unfortunately (and by Ethan Hawke, publicly at an awards ceremony, my best shot at any kind of actual notoriety), Ander Manson. There's your notoriety. That these names refer to the same personage is not in dispute.

Pending deletion and discussion of it, I am thinking about where I belong, whether in Wikipedia or not, or if that's a decision I'm qualified to make. I am thinking about where I fit in the continuum of Wikipedia inclusionists—again, those who argue for more things to be included on Wikipedia, notable or not, who are essentially arguing in favor of subjectivity—and deletionists, those who argue for objectivity. It's a worldview, I figure, an ethos, a choice of two or somewhere in between.

It doesn't take long. While searching for more Ander Monson–related material, I enter a whole new world of Ander (non-Monson) in which we rapidly become a multiplicity. Monsons are not crazy unusual—see the mudflaps on occasional trucks that read, with red circles for the Os, MONSON, being apparently a trucking or freight company. When I see these trucks, they make me feel a little bit less alone. Also less singular, the downside of not being alone.

Ander IV:

Ander Alert is the title of a "new local blog for Florida's Fourth Congressional District and Watching the Actions of Andrew Crenshaw," who inexplicably goes by Ander rather than what appears to be his given name, Andrew (according only to this unofficial blog devoted to him: I have seen him addressed as "Andrew" nowhere else), making him only the fourth Ander I have ever even heard of.

Ander II:

I was contacted by Ander II in college. He was Swedish. He did not speak English very well. We talked via email briefly and were pleased to have met another Ander. For those with unusual names (though really, it's not that outlandish, not an X or a Y or anything), the world can appear to be a lonely or solipsistic place.[†] In this moment we achieved solidarity, oneness. In this universe we were no longer alone.

Ander IV:

Ander Crenshaw, of the website[†] *Ander Alert,* looks like a genial guy, American flag in the background of his photo reproduced on the anti-Ander blog.

Titles of individual posts (that usefully apply also to this Ander, your author) include:

"Ander Thinks We're Stupid" (07/04/08)

"Ander Hates America and Its Values" (06/28/08)

"Ander Is Wasting Your Time in Washington" (06/28/08)

"Ander Joins Bi-Partisan Crime Syndicate to Obstruct Justice" (06/20/08)

"Ander Has a Good Job—Tough Luck if You Don't" (06/13/08)

"Ander Says Our Laws Are For Sale . . . Sells Out 4th Amendment" (06/11/08)

"Ander Hates the Environment" (02/24/08)

"Ander Loves Bush" (10/05/07)

"Ander Hates Children and the Elderly" (08/15/07)

. . . and the anticlimactic "Ander Crenshaw Resources" (08/13/07)

I don't think I can overstate the weirdness of seeing the name Ander in bold type at the top of a congressman's official website. Like a reported 33 percent of Americans, I am used to periodically self-Googling, a term so often used that it has become a little bit of a cliché, almost, especially for writerly types. I got to this page while only Googling "Ander," which brought up the awesomely named *Ander Alert,* which I had assumed was perhaps designed to keep a watchful eye on the alleged molesterish or lecherous tendencies of yours truly. Alas. But I am proud of our congressman Ander. One of us has broken through. He is notable. He has a Wikipedia page. No one is arguing for its deletion.

Ander III:

Actually I ran across another Ander (bagging both iterations III and IV on the same day on my hunt for more of me, thirteen years after encountering iteration II, and following an obviously long history with iteration I) reading an article on the blog the *Consumerist,* which is one of four blogs I regularly read in the mornings while trying to ease myself into the caffeinated dawn. I imagine the writer Gary Snyder would find this sad, that I reach for my laptop and read online for a while, answer an email or two, maybe, once I get going. He's opposed to that kind of immediacy—or perhaps I should call it intermediaricy. I asked him, when he recently visited the college where I taught, whether he reads his own reviews, or whether he self-Googles, a term that I had to explain. Perhaps he just wanted to humiliate me. He is a cruel man. He probably gets up and contemplates the pines and the breeze and the eroding earth for an hour, not that I have anything against Snyder, pines, or breeze, or eroding earth. I support all three.

The *Consumerist* article indicates that a guy named Ander (last name unknown) from Florida (hmm) is being stiffed by Blue Cross Blue Shield of Florida for a "bi-lateral arthroplasty on [his] jaw for TMJ." Oddly, he lives in Florida with Ander number IV, and more oddly TMJ is possibly in my future, according to a dentist I saw while in high school. I also had a recently denied medical claim (like how many Americans, I wonder) as discussed in "Voir Dire" earlier in this book.[†] All this amounts to a lot of Ander in a short time period, itself a sort of Ander Alert.

If you care, when Googling Ander, my name comes up as number 10 on the first page of Google. By the time you read this, it will have changed.

Andr.net is some sort of semibogus hacker site last updated in 2004, but still somehow persisting.

As *ander* is German (and Dutch) for *other,* I am interested in these other Anders who are others with me, ourselves outside the traditional lineage of naming. There are tens of thousands of people named Anders, including my grandfather, for whom I am slightly misnamed.

Ander V:

Even better is *Ander's Homoworld,* being the blog of "a 27 year old gay guy exploring London and other countries where to spend our young lives before committing ourselves to a live [*sic*] with responsibilities and babies." This is a great little mouthful in itself. My father was quite sure I was gay for some time in college, and I get this quite a bit from people. I sang tenor 2 and have a predilection for karaokeing songs across gender, which means, what, exactly, I wonder?

You Megans and Roberts and Jaclyns and Walters know what it's like to encounter your names every day, but for us Anders it is a new experience. I am constantly rediscovering things in the world. Thanks to the splendors of Internet search, it's a quick trip to the website for Ander, Texas, a pre–Civil War town originally named Hanover. There are no connections here to be found, unlike with all the other Anders. It is, like so many things, a dead end[†].

Inevitably on page six of the Google results we get "Pamela Ander Porn Videoson," and I'm finally connected to that most famous of leaked sex tapes—and the beginning of the sex tape era and the end of any sense that our sex or other lives are private anymore.

Ander VI:

Each new Ander I find now—and they are starting to proliferate quite quickly (an Ander Kase, a "happily married professional artist living the artist's life" in California, for instance), enlarging my world of possible and in fact probable and increasingly concrete Anders, by powers of two, shrinking me down to the level of everybody else's sense of submersion, submission to their parents' whatever wishes in choosing their name. This Ander Kase posts the following: "I got a notice regarding my 30-year high school reunion. I've yet to attend any of these 'self-promoting,' 'gossip mongering,' 'clique-ish' forums. I choose to be part of the blogosphere instead." This language is attached to his untitled abstract painting from 1975 (the year I was born, according to Wikipedia) featured on his blog. The image is quite beautiful—it belongs in space,[†] an image of an exploding nebula maybe, diffuse for now, quadrillions of tiny particles that appear as a cloud, which will eventually be condensed into a star.

Ander VII, a bit of a reach:

The character Samuel Anders, in the Sci-Fi Channel's recent stellar iteration of the television show *Battlestar Galactica,* finds himself, in the season three finale, to be a Cylon, a sentient and infinitely reproducible human-looking robot (to gloss the situation awkwardly). It's complicated, like most sci-fi, but Cylons are machines made by humans. In the original campy version of the series, televised in the seventies, evil one-eyed man-made Cylons battled humans for some reason or other, before being defeated, and disappearing. In the new show, which takes place years into the future, the Cylons return, but they have invented a new breed of Cylons that impersonate humans. Anders is one of them. He has memories, looks human, acts human, thinks he is human, and in every way seems human— but he is one of thirteen models, and doesn't know it, a sleeper agent, biding time until a switch goes off somewhere, and he is awakened into a new world where he is no longer an individual—or so he thinks. (The truth of the show is more complicated, and is about individuality and humanity and identity, which is what makes it a good show, an interesting human drama set in space.) He is now one of many. He is connected. He is related. But inside the one, the brain, is the many, the lineage, the thousand iterations of Anders, all emanating, one imagines, from an original Anders, the prototype, the mold from which the others have been made. This question eventually shows up toward the end of the series: there are originals, in a sense, of each model. And this spawns other questions: if there is an original, what does this do to the sense of communal identity? To ownership of consciousness[†]? To individuality? Does the original get to feel superior? Is that wrong?

This I is a solo I in the middle of thousands of these Is, all perking up with what they have to say, asserting themselves via blog, or via blog asserting itself against them and their actions, their existence. I inside of I. Unlike many characters, the letter I, in caps at least, is infinitely scalable. Being symmetrical, you can reproduce one inside another, inside another, inside another. The series could shrink and decrease and still be geometrically similar. Each letterform I contains or suggests the mold for an infinite number of others, dependent only on how much metal type you have or how large your computer can render the image. The lowercase i does not have this quality. It is also scalable but cannot physically contain the millions of other lowercases. But when I erects and broadcasts itself, it takes the stage, the cake, the stage name: it is awakened and, awkward at first, it starts to stride forward, make some statements, support some presidents, hate the elderly, become an impressionist landscape painter leaving that old abstract art behind. It gets sentient, starts Googling itself, seeing how many there are of it. As for *ander*, Google lists "about" thirty-eight million hits. The number was determined by the server farms on which Google's arithmetic algorithmed it out in .09 seconds. About the length of time it would take to strike one character on the computer keyboard.

I have little interest in making contact with these other Anders. It's not that I don't want to reduce my loneliness by touching another made from the same mold (however we'd like to think that names are not a stamp, a mark of similarity, I believe they are, especially the more obscure ones, where fewer of us share the mantle). But I also don't want to pierce the shell of my own I, to touch the edge of what it means to be an Ander, an I, Ander, to have an alert sent out, or at least blogged occasionally, for me.

Ander VIII:

Ander ranks the 8,807th most sexy and the 16,848th most popular of the 91,923 celebrities on the website *The Celebrity Ranker*. This refers, pleasingly (?), to Ander Page[†], a porn star, whose MySpace page indicates that she is "pretty much into most things except interracial and gang bang scenes . . . [she] like[s] to keep [her] girlish image." I would like to echo that emotion. I added her as a friend and asked the same. She has not followed suit. Yet. Does this mean I have to download one of her sex tapes? These are the staged type of sex tapes, which don't map to what we mean when we say sex tape, really—meaning not having the verisimilitude, the immediacy of the Pamela Anderson tape, or the Fred Durst tape, or the Paris Hilton tape— though the recent trend toward "homemade" or homemade, or amateur sex tapes in professional porn, appears to capitalize on this trend, which coincides with porn stars assuming names similar to the famous Hilton or "Puma Swede," a hoax advertisement for Puma brand shoes with implicit oral sex that has been much discussed and reproduced online—and there are now sexual variations of YouTube devoted specifically to adult content, Xtube being the only one I've spent any time on—or should I omit that? The comments on Ander Page's MySpace are just bizarre. Here is a sample: "Hey beutifull [*sic*] shust [*sic*] wanted to comment on how fine u are love'd [*sic*] your movie down the hatch" and "Have a great 4'th [*sic*] !!! Paul says Bang Hard!!!" Her MySpace friends are maybe the single saddest bunch of people (us nonporn Anders included) I have ever laid eyes on, virtually. I can only imagine them in person, though they would surely never assemble unless invited by Ander Page, perhaps for a fivesome, to be filmed for streaming online. *A Confluence of Anders* doesn't sound that sexy. Maybe *Ander Alert* would work.

The more Anders we run across the less Ander begins to mean, to sound in the hollows of the mouth. The same goes for the iteration of the MySpace/Facebook version of friend, who often enough, as we all know, are not really friends. MySpace offers us the options to "Browse Friends, Find Friends, Invite Friends," among others on the Friends Menu. The fact that there is even a friends menu tells us something about what it means to have friends or "friends" today.

There is the I that sets up the I's MySpace or other social networking page, creating an avatar, a projected I that is essentially fictional, or at the least a persona. Here's how I describe myself to you, it says. These are my favorite songs. These are my favorite bands. These are my favorite books. These are my friends and what they wrote on my wall. From this constellation of data emerges an apparent I. That I connects to other Is and they have interactions. Line them up on the fence like gourds, public layer painted on public layer. Cut each open and you'll see rings of paint, of layers, of projections, each older, more thoughtful I layered on the next, having removed the indiscreet party photographs, having buried the correspondence with the former lover, discarded most of those old notes, having excised as much as we think possible of that previous candy-colored shell of self.

We will return to those selves[†] later, as our older friends contact us on Facebook, as we go to our high school reunions, as we run into people who knew the old us on the street and force us back into our old selves, if only for a moment.

Ander Page (also apparently known sometimes as Ander Paige) is the blankest page, the biggest shell of the bunch, the zestiest nacho cheese Dorito fantasy you can buy. Porn stars craft (or have chosen for them) their own names, personas, the desires they want to represent. They are dolls, pliable, easy, fake, fantastic, seemingly substantial. They do what you want them to do. They might do you. They are unattainable. Inside them could be anything: for instance, the artist Ander Kane (itself a sort of porny name) painting beautiful frescoes on the inside of the doll-shell of Ander Page. Being inside an Ander must be beautiful, a dark, other space, infinitely customizable, with joints that articulate in no less than twenty places. Inside the shell of Ander Kane is un-last-named-in-the-way-of-blogs-with-their-faux-private-worlds Homo Ander, who defines himself as gay first. Before being Ander, he is first homo. And he constructs the world in his image. I am happy to live inside Homo Ander as a homunculus, no less animatronic than most dolls in spite of being driven by sorcery, an external manifestation of desire, perhaps. I don't imagine that I am the central Ander. Or, I don't any longer; I imagine thousands of Anders floating in bubbles through space, each redecorating our interior space with physical wallpaper, or digital wallpaper like those used as backgrounds on your laptop screens or as backgrounds on your social network residences.

—

The sky above me—night, midnight, more or less, quiet and dreamy in the outside air—moves quickly, clouds as wallpaper, as background, or maybe as foreground to the blacker background where we have projected our myths on stars to make meaning of them.

It is beautiful, though, and we project our myths on names: my response to a Timothy, say, is colored by all the previous Timothys I have known, that I may have disliked intensely, so Timothy for me is a name, too timorous and obtuse to get very far in life, of people that I am more likely to dislike. How about the Anders there? Does my self-regard extend to them? Does my self-loathing? If we were to meet, what would occur?

Ander IX:

I don't want to ruminate too long on names, because names are shells, shells inside shells found half-buried in the sand. My *Dungeons & Dragons* counterpart is Ander Goodchild, a human priest of Farlaghan, whatever that is. He is an NPC (non-player character, a character that the player may not play as, but might encounter on his travels through a digital gamespace) in the *D&D* game system version 3.5. He exists, sort of, as a prop in an ongoing fictional world.

MySpace (or Facebook, or any other social networking site) forces us to play a character, to choose which Ander to play, to present to the world. Ander editor, teacher, writer, job hunter, disc golfer, lawn mower, husband, douchebag, authoritarian, ironist, Dungeon Master, etc. All resolve, in practice, to the same physical body (typing, enjoying the night and the clouds and the breeze), but in practice they are quite different and are played differently in various games.

The Amazon search-inside-the-book function (for books whose publishers or authors have expressly permitted this) allows you to search and read inside any book on Amazon. More interestingly, though, Amazon applies a set of algorithms to the text, making a concordance (you can see the top one hundred words an author uses in the book), assessing the readability level (in comparison to all the other books Amazon can access, though you can limit this by restricting it to memoirs, or books of literary essays, or whatever). It reduces the author to a set of numbers, which is what we are anyhow, a set of responses to stimuli and networked pathways in the brain. It's likely that we are not as individual as we would like to think, if we can only get deep enough inside the physiology of the mind to understand this.

Tourist in my former hometown, staying at a Days Hotel downtown (the nouveau take on the Days Inn chain, reserved for the more upscale of the set), I see a different city.† I can almost see my former house up on the ridge that ascends away from the Grand River. I am in the hotel, the opposite of a local, more than a little lonely, having an out-of-city experience. I eat breakfast at a place I'd never tried when I lived here. On the plane I sit next to a woman who I could only presume from her dress and demeanor was a porn star. It is possible Ander Page was sitting in 9-B (exit row, since the porn stars get a slight upgrade from coach and can be used as flotation devices in a pinch). If this is true, then that puts two of us Anders, a binary star, in one metal shell moving over the earth.

Sure it's unlikely. She was beautiful in a similarly unlikely way. Not dressed up completely but her body seemed out of place on a plane traveling into Michigan. I wanted—as I had wanted as an adolescent—the ability to see inside people's minds. We know from reading science fiction that this gift, like any other, eventually leads to ruin. I wanted to know how close this Ander Page was to me, how close I was to a celebrity, or a woman who had left her celebrity behind her, traveling coach back to Michigan, giving up on updating her professional MySpace page, wanting, perhaps, no longer to play that role, to make that space her space. Instead we shared the space. We shared my laptop light. There was nothing otherwise notable about the flight. I look for meaning in everything. I can almost proposition the woman next to me, or at least start a conversation. People on planes used to always chat with me, but this hasn't happened for a couple of years now. My demeanor must be different. I must be a different form of Ander, another layer of the ball. I'm not sure what else I can say about it.

VANISHING POINT: MIDDLE WEST, CITIZENSHIP

The Midwest, which is to say the debate about what the Midwest is or contains (Missouri? North[†] Dakota? Pennsylvania? Nebraska?), which is to say part of the section between the coasts, the middle before you get to the West, is about transit. It is transitional. We know this caught in mile-long streams of traffic and trucks queueing up behind and beside another, three wide at times, to transport materials or goods from one place[†] to another, through the middle of the country. Though this space,[†] this horizontality, would appear to be static, with the small towns where little seems to change, or so television tells us, and everyone moves slowly and drinks at the same bars day in and out—what appears to be a static equilibrium, a balanced equation—it is still all about transition, from one place to another. It is for us at this moment, driving from small college to small college in our rented Ford Escape, escaping from little, escaping to little, incapable of any real sort of escape, if we wanted to attempt it, having no skills to speak of, and loving the world enough to continue wanting all of it, Hungry Hungry Hippo style, coveting it in all its glory and variety. We are in the metal exoskeleton of the car, iPod playing familiar music through the speakers (and the world accordingly transforming itself cartoonlike as in a number of television commercials for mp3 players—the world can be made over, our experience transformed, as easy as this via soundtrack), climate control set to keep us at a temperature we are used to, electric seating system positioned for the idea of comfort: we are as *at home* as is possible in a rental, transitional car. Normally we have our Sirius satellite radio, which allows us to bypass the horror of local programming for a glistening network of channels beamed down to us from space, no less. But this time the iPod is deployed, projecting our own soundtrack for our trip, our life, the *we* in wePod (the collective consciousness[†] of music lists and listeners), everywhere around us, even in the air. We have the GPS plugged in, too, so there's no need for maps, and the whole idea of being lost is now entirely quaint (which is a sadness because we like the darkness of the unexplored map, but we are practical: we also want to get there and back quickly, and besides we can see the world passing by in real time as we drive via GPS, the names of roads and rivers and golf courses; we could almost drive with the GPS only and not pay attention to the actual world around us, but technology hasn't got us there quite yet). We are self-sufficient. Located. In command. An American dream. An orgasm on the move. It is really fucking great.

We are driving back from the World's Biggest Ball[†] of Paint where we painted coat #21,406, a nice cerulean sort of Sherwin-Williams blue. We donated to the cause and received a couple of chips that had been shaved off the Ball that demonstrate hundreds of paint layers, concentric circles originally, until gravity and sloppy paint jobs and individuality distorted its shape (it's surely more vertical than horizontal now). Sherwin-Williams sponsors it and (we believe this is what the proprietors said) built the barn in which the Ball is now housed, dangling from an industrial-looking set of steel beams and cable from the ceiling. Sherwin-Williams also donates all the paint. In return the corporate logo is displayed behind the Ball ("Sherwin-Williams: Cover the Earth!"). In this way Mike and Glenda Carmichael, creators and tenders of the Ball, have put the town on the map.

Alexandria, Indiana, might have been in danger of vanishing otherwise. We drove by a lot of abandoned buildings, including some huge complexes where things were once warehoused, refined, produced, or packaged, with the requisite shattered windows, graffiti, rusting machinery, plant life returning through all that space. We have no doubt that in a generation it will be subsumed entirely. It will be gone, and the memory[†] of it will have to persist since it will be out of view, postapocalyptic. We don't know if the Ball is an example of Mike and Glenda's substantially engaging with the world, or if our visiting it is a substantial engagement (something to which we aspire as readers and explorers), or if both are a fiction, a regression from that kind of engagement. The Ball is beautiful. Mike and Glenda are proud. They also seem a little tired (Glenda has done nine thousand plus of the coats herself). We worked up a sweat painting it (it's now become very large), so we can only imagine.

The Ball is the reverse of vanishing. It grows larger every day. We helped to enlarge it, took part, became citizens of the Ball. It has inspired, or co-incided with, other balls. Another Alexandrian, Andy Cunningham, is in the process of making what he hopes will eventually become the world's largest biggest ball of plastic wrap. And a few years back, Alexandria was in the news for pulling a four hundred–pound hairball out of the sewer. It has since dissolved, but the town built a replica, which is featured in the town's annual Christmas parade.

Oddly, the Department of Homeland Security has reportedly identified the Ball of Paint as a "distinguished heritage site," which requires funds for terror defense.

A couple of filmmakers made a documentary about the Ball four years ago but it was never distributed or released, though there's a slick website.[†] Mike is miffed that the filmmakers never showed the film in Alexandria, or even to the two of them, though it premiered, apparently, in Boston. And ended there. One imagines the film did not depict the Ball or the town or the denizens of it all that kindly.

If you go to see the Ball (or at least on the website you can see it by proxy, like 493,146 of your fellow Internetters), drive east along Washington Street on your way back out of Alexandria. See if you can see the ruins or if they are now gone. Stop in at JW's, a tiny bar that serves domestic bottles on Fridays for a buck (their selection is, as you'd imagine, limited). They also have tacos. The front window looks across at the ruins. No one in the bar is going anywhere anytime soon. But you are. You are driving through to see the Ball, to sign the guest book,[†] have your picture taken, touch a legend, paint the Ball, become part of history, say that you've done that, and then you're gone on to something else, the World's Biggest Pecan, maybe, in Missouri, or the World's Biggest Crucifix, in Michigan. But they are there. And the Ball—and the building and the thinking that contains the Ball (as if anything could really contain the Ball!)—will be tended gracefully. And it continues to expand. Because of you. And you. Because of all of us.

SOLIPSISM[1]

Being the theory that the self is the only thing that can be known and verified. Maybe this is memoir after all in spite of my kicking against the pricks of it.

Me. Me. Me. Me. Me. Me. Me. Me. Me. Me. Me. Me. Me. Me. Me. Me. Me.
Me. Me. Me. Me. Me. Me. Me. Me. Me. Me. Me. Me. Me. Me. Me. Me. Me.
Me. Me. Me. Me. Me. Me. Me. Me. Me. Me. Me. Me. Me. Me. Me. Me. Me.
Me. Me. Me. Me. Me. Me. Me. Me. Me. Me. Me. Me. Me. Me. Me. Me. Me.
Me. Me. Me. Me. Me. Me. Me. Me. Me. Me. Me. Me. Me. Me. Me. Me. Me.
Me. Me. Me. Me. Me. Me. Me. Me. Me. Me. Me. Me. Me. Me. Me. Me. Me.
Me. Me. Me. Me. Me. Me. Me. Me. Me. Me. Me. Me. Me. Me. Me. Me. Me.
Me. Me. Me. Me. Me. Me. Me. Me. Me. Me. Me. Me. Me. Me. Me. Me. Me.
Me. Me. Me. Me. Me. Me. Me. Me. Me. Me. Me. Me. Me. Me. Me. Me. Me.
Me. Me. Me. Me. Me. Me. Me. Me. Me. Me. Me. Me. Me. Me. Me. Me. Me.
Me. Me. Me. Me. Me. Me. Me. Me. Me. Me. Me. Me. Me. Me. Me. Me. Me.
Me. Me. Me. Me. Me. Me. Me. Me. Me. Me. Me. Me. Me. Me. Me. Me. Me.
Me. Me. Me. Me. Me. Me. Me. Me. Me. Me. Me. Me. Me. Me. Me. Me. Me.
Me. Me.[†] Me. Me. Me. Me. Me. Me. Me. Me. Me. Me. Me. Me. Me. Me. Me.
Me. Me. Me. Me. Me. Me. Me. Me. Me. Me. Me. Me. Me. Me. Me. Me. Me.
Me. Me. Me. Me. Me. Me. Me. Me. Me. Me. Me. Me. Me. Me. Me. Me. Me.
Me. Me. Me. Me. Me. Me. Me. Me. Me. Me. Me. Me. Me. Me. Me. Me. Me.
Me. Me. Me. Me. Me. Me. Me. Me. Me. Me. Me. Me. Me. Me. Me. Me. Me.
Me. Me. Me. Me. Me. Me. Me. Me. Me. Me. Me. Me. Me. Me. Me. Me. Me.
Me. Me. Me. Me. Me. Me. Me. Me. Me. Me. Me. Me. Me. Me. Me. Me. Me.

Me. Me. Me. Me. Me. Me. Me. Me. Me. Me. Me. Me. Me. Me. Me. Me.
Me. Me. Me. Me. Me. Me. Me. Me. Me. Me. Me. Me. Me. Me. Me. Me.
Me. Me. Me. Me. Me. Me. Me. Me. Me. Me. Me. Me. Me. Me. Me. Me.
Me. Me. Me. Me. Me. Me. Me. Me. Me. Me. Me. Me. Me. Me. Me. Me.
Me. Me. Me. Me. Me. Me. Me. Me. Me. Me. Me. Me. Me. Me. Me. Me.
Me. Me. Me. Me. Me. Me. Me. Me. Me. Me. Me. Me. Me. Me. Me. Me.
Me. Me. Me. Me. Me. Me. Me. Me. Me. Me. Me. Me. Me. Me. Me. Me.
Me. Me. Me. Me. Me. Me. Me. Me. Me. Me. Me. Me. Me. Me. Me. Me.
Me. Me. Me. Me. Me. Me. Me. Me. Me. Me. Me. Me. Me. Me. Me. Me.
Me. Me. Me. Me. Me. Me. Me. Me. Me. Me. Me. Me. Me. Me. Me. Me.
Me. Me. Me. Me. Me. Me. Me. Me. Me. Me. Me. Me. Me. Me. Me. Me.
Me. Me. Me. Me. Me. Me. Me. Me. Me. Me. Me. Me. Me. Me. Me. Me.
Me. Me. Me. Me. Me. Me. Me. Me. Me. Me. Me. Me. Me. Me. Me. Me.
Me. Me. Me. Me. Me. Me. Me. Me. Me. Me. Me. Me. Me. Me. Me. Me.
Me. Me. Me. Me. Me. Me. Me. Me. Me. Me. Me. Me. Me. Me. Me. Me.
Me. Me. Me. Me. Me. Me. Me. Me. Me. Me. Me. Me. Me. Me. Me. Me.
Me. Me. Me. Me. Me. Me. Me. Me. Me. Me. Me. Me. Me. Me. Me. Me.
Me. Me. Me. Me. Me. Me. Me. Me. Me. Me. Me. Me. Me. Me. Me. Me.
Me. Me. Me. Me. Me. Me. Me. Me. Me. Me. Me. Me. Me. Me. Me. Me.
Me. Me. Me. Me. Me. Me. Me. Me. Me. Me. Me. Me. Me. Me. Me. Me.
Me. Me. Me. Me. Me. Me. Me. Me. Me. Me. Me. Me. Me. Me. Me. Me.
Me. Me. Me. Me. Me. Me. Me. Me. Me. Me. Me. Me. Me. Me. Me. Me.
Me. Me. Me. Me. Me. Me. Me. Me. Me. Me. Me. Me. Me. Me. Me. Me.
Me. Me. Me. Me. Me. Me. Me. Me. Me. Me. Me. Me. Me. Me. Me. Me.
Me. Me. Me. Me. Me. Me. Me. Me. Me. Me. Me. Me. Me. Me. Me. Me.
Me. Me. Me. Me. Me. Me. Me. Me. Me. Me. Me. Me. Me. Me. Me. Me.
Me. Me. Me. Me. Me. Me. Me. Me. Me. Me. Me. Me. Me. Me. Me. Me.
Me. Me. Me. Me. Me. Me. Me. Me. Me. Me. Me. Me. Me. Me. Me. Me.
Me. Me. Me. Me. Me. Me. Me. Me. Me. Me. Me. Me. Me. Me. Me. Me.
Me. Me. Me. Me. Me. Me. Me. Me. Me. Me. Me. Me. Me. Me. Me. Me.
Me. Me. Me. Me. Me. Me. Me. Me. Me. Me. Me. Me. Me. Me. Me. Me.
Me. Me. Me. Me. Me. Me. Me. Me. Me. Me. Me. Me. Me. Me. Me. Me.
Me. Me. Me. Me. Me. Me. Me. Me. Me. Me. Me. Me. Me. Me. Me. Me.
Me. Me. Me. Me. Me. Me. Me. Me. Me. Me. Me. Me. Me. Me. Me. Me.
Me. Me. Me. Me. Me. Me. Me. Me. Me. Me. Me. Me. Me. Me. Me. Me.
Me. Me. Me. Me. Me. Me. Me. Me. Me. Me. Me. Me. Me. Me. Me. Me.
Me. Me. Me. Me. Me. Me. Me. Me. Me. Me. Me. Me. Me. Me. Me. Me.
Me. Me. Me. Me. Me. Me. Me. Me. Me. Me. Me. Me. Me. Me. Me. Me.
Me. Me. Me. Me. Me. Me. Me. Me. Me. Me. Me. Me. Me. Me. Me. Me.
Me. Me. Me. Me. Me. Me. Me. Me. Me. Me. Me. Me. Me. Me. Me. Me.

*

At one point, say, the late 1800s, just before Thomas Edison, or James Fields Smathers, or the Blickensderfer Manufacturing Company invents the electric typewriter, this would have meant more than it does today. That is, the 1,003 instances of *Me.* above—and don't forget the single space[†] after each period, which means another keystroke for each instance[2]—would have meant significantly more in 1895 than it does today. Physically speaking, the work required to generate the instances above on a manual typewriter, where you'd have to press each key hard enough to get the system of levers moving the type bar through an inked ribbon to hit the paper, was far greater than the work it required to generate this page on a computer. One reason people get carpal tunnel now is because the physical act of typing (itself lessened by about 95 percent in electric typewriters as compared to manuals, and now computer keyboards reduce that even further) doesn't require as much work now as it did then, so it's easier for the hands to become lazy and just rest, and for us not to arch our fingers enough, etc.

It would have taken me, in eighth grade, when I typed fifty-four words per minute in our class just recently rechristened *keyboarding*[†] instead of the older *typing*, approximately 18.6 minutes to generate that page, probably longer when you think about the fatigue that sets in typing the same letters over and over—no variety of motion at all, just simple repetition—and of course this was on an electric typewriter, not even one of the old manual machines.

For me now it took less than thirty seconds to compose that text. I typed "Me. Me. Me." on my Titanium 15″ PowerBook keyboard, which isn't all that comfortable, really, though I've gotten used to it because of the ease it otherwise affords, and then

Invents is a fuzzy verb of course—often so-called inventions aren't a lightning-strike kind of moment but the latest in a series of incremental increases in existing technologies just significant enough to be seen as something completely, more or less inarguably, new.

Work is equal to force times distance, remember.

Already the apparent persistence of the Titanium 15″ PowerBook keyboard (or at least its name—is there any highlighted in Dreamweaver,[3] copy-and-pasted a few times until I had a few lines, then copy-and-pasted that a few times, and came up with a good solid page of text, all text about me with a capital M in front trailed by a period and space. It's almost nothing. I didn't have to think about it, the *Me.* or the actual Me much. It's easy to do. You try it.

So how much does it mean? What work does it do given that it took vastly fewer minutes, calluses, and calories?

—

I make broadsides, mostly pretty artistic, fine-press sorts of productions, for poetry and fiction readings at Grand Valley State University, the college that currently employs me. I don't know if anyone really cares that these broadsides get made or not as a condition of my employment, so I do them out of a love of the artifact of the broadside, the mementos that they are, and the simple beauty of elegantly typeset lines of prose or verse. Mostly I do these by offset printer (printing press) or by laser printer in my office. I don't handset the type for a Vandercook letterpress, though I have done that too. When you're handsetting every letter, pulling them out of the type cases, which are sort of strangely arranged, and setting them in lines, you have a lot of time to think about the process of production, and about the words you are laboring over. The type of course appears reversed on the page from how it appears to you, so certain letters are very easy to confuse (hence the saying "mind your p's and q's"), so it's a maddening and painstaking, somehow beautiful process to print like this. You get to experience the physical act of print production, and this kind of letterpress work is now an extravagance, incurring

actual titanium in it? I have doubts) is on the wane. This essay is revised two computers later, on a MacBookPro G5. The old electronic case has been returned and surely scrapped with all its data and its physical memory,[†] the accumulated finger oil rubbed all across its keyboard (no lie! the keyboard was grimy when I was done with it, presumably with leavings from the body).

Formerly employed me, now, technically, since this text has been now retranscribed and enshrined in text, since I now (inasmuch as saying *now* accomplishes anything at all, though I suppose it argues for the eternal now at the point of its composition (whatever *that* means, since the text has been recomposed a number of times), the literary present tense) teach at the University of Arizona (where David Foster Wallace got his MFA, as I am constantly reminded), where I am not asked to do anything design-related, which makes me, I admit, a little sad, since it splits my self in half (again (again again)).

significant expense. Try to get your wedding invitations letterpressed and you'll find out.

I do most of my design in Adobe InDesign, which takes care of a lot for you. For instance, it automatically kerns (spaces) prose, and handles line breaks and widows and orphans, mostly, and the sorts of details typographers love, like ligatures and old style figures, and all of that. I can turn on those options if I'm using a good OpenType typeface and let it do its thing. I print these broadsides in an edition of fifty to five hundred normally, depending, for writers like Charles Wright, Charles Baxter, and I hope someday to do Charles Yu, thus completing my trilogy of Charleses. Also Rita Dove, Sonia Sanchez, David Means, and so on. Sometimes I'll finish them with a deckle or ragged edge, or by burning the edges of the broadsides for effect. I always wanted to put a set in a stack, bring it to a firing range, and shoot through it for a really cool effect. I might use some spray-on fixer or a cheaper analog like hairspray to keep the toner from dusting off on hands and slacks. I have thrown red wine across broadsides for effect. And applied rubber stamps. Spray painted. Even printed with my own blood. The list goes on.

Ain't I fancy? Is this essay about me? Is all nonfiction about the me, the I, the eye trained in on the self?

I did one broadside for the writer Mark Ehling at the University of Alabama by laser-printing fake reproduction letterhead on a nice cotton paper and then hand-typing the text on one of the few coveted, rare now, manual typewriters in the university. I did about eighty using this method. Each time I would make mistakes and either go back and XXX them out or just type over them, throw on some new line breaks (the piece was prose, so it didn't matter as much what the text block looked like), and make each broadside a completely different production. By the time I was halfway through I knew Mark's work, a couple of short paragraphs, intimately. I began to hate them, to hate him for writing them, and to hate Mr. Edison, or the inventor of the specific model I was using, an IBM Selectric, for putting me in this position. There was also some self-loathing.

What I'm trying to say, though, is that each broadside I did that way meant more than the other ones I do offset, by the hundred (though they're all still individually numbered by hand: this is essential to the making of the art object, the collectible). Maybe not to the average reader who sees it, says *cool*, and takes it home folded up (maddening!), or leaves it there, but for me, certainly, and for the writer (maybe), and for the act of production, of channeling the text, of this kind of re-creation, a corollary artistic act, an act of speaking out, of selfhood, of assertion.

I have a lot of semi-thought-out theories about the mechanisms of production writers have used, and about how (or whether) the technologies they used (longhand, dictation, typewriter, Microsoft Word, Pagemaker, Dreamweaver, InDesign, Flash, etc.) affected the work they did. I'm a little too lazy to go very far with that conceit in terms of busting out my close reading and LitCrit chops and such, but it's a salient point. (For one, I think we could probably do something with Marxist criticism and this idea of work: maybe an essay for another day.) As for me, I am writing this essay in a program that specializes in bringing together these different formats of items (images: GIF, JPEG, PNG; interactive stuff like Flash and Shockwave buttons; sound; movie clips; text; hyperlinks; JavaScript and other programming elements) in a WYSIWYG format. I wonder how this affects the words I am writing—do they mean less, or more, or something different? What if I process my words through a Shockwave digital effect so they can flash or something? Does that change the words and make them something different, something beyond words? Words marked up with formatting? And what does *writing* consist of, exactly?

What you see is what you get is how the acronym works, a technology not really possible until word processing programs like Microsoft Word, originally called "Multi-Tool Word," began to be able to display fonts onscreen as they would actually appear, which takes a surprising amount of processing power and still does not work flawlessly.

Especially weird is the thought that this essay is being created for the web only, not for the page, with no thought of 8.5 x 11 inch paper (or in Europe the A4 sheet) with the standard margins that Word thinks acceptable, or the other constraints (or pleasures—this goes both ways, as many people don't like reading longer texts onscreen, and love the feeling of crisp new paper in their hands) of the page. I

Far weirder still is the fact that this essay was anthologized in *The Best American Essays 2008*, a series that I formerly took cheap shots at for its apparent conservatism; so this transient, translucent, ruminating thing written on the am also not editing it in the same way, given that it is available on the website[†] for free. You didn't pay for this. It's an extra. A promotional item, maybe. Or an attempt to extend the idea of what a book[†] can do in an explicit way. And as it's here for you, it's like the opposite of solipsism, a piece of writing explicitly intended as communication. It's like getting your own personalized email from me to you, except that I don't have your email address, and you'd probably just delete it out of hand as spam anyhow.

Or maybe it's a bonus[†] for the portion of readers who go online to get more out of a book, having been burned before by the lameness of promotional websites for books that should have great websites, like Mark Z. Danielewski's *House of Leaves*—I am writing this for you, dear reader who just wants more. Or maybe it's like the bonus materials/special features you find on DVDs that mostly—let's admit it now—suck, are useless, in spite of the promises made by proponents of the technology.

Now DVDs have this space, and viewers do expect the extras. Sometimes they are great, like Peter Jackson's work on the *Lord of the Rings* trilogy, or in my awesome (and I mean that—it inspires awe, even in the packaging) *Alien Quadrilogy* DVD set (nine DVDs, two cuts of each movie plus a pile of bonus stuff, and amazing foldout packaging—the artifact of it is sexy as all hell, a design miracle). And sometimes they are not. But consumers want those extras. And now CDs that come packaged with videos, multimedia stuff, some live tracks, an extra DVD for fans who care enough not to simply download them on the Internet.

web for the web about writing on the web and for the web, so it's now been re-enshrined in print three times (more on this in an endnote), first in the literary magazine the *Pinch*, then in *BAE*, and now in this book. I'm re-re-reprinting it in this text because it echoes a number of the ideas about self and production and process and absorption that this book is also about, and plus, it was totally in *Best American Essays,* so I am hoping to convince my editors at Graywolf that I am a force to be reckoned with by its inclusion and my self-consciousness about it, about the authorial and editing process, about everything, really, from my clothes and my weight and my unripped abs, my receding hairline, penchant for drunkery, and my crappy programming styles in Pascal and C++ in college and even, eh, whatever—I could follow this trail forever if I don't stop myself, pull out from the recursive spiral, huzzah! I would also add that this is a strangely casual essay, caused no doubt by my not writing it for "publication," which freed me up to do a bunch of things I might not otherwise do. Though, in the version for this artifact I have peeled back some of the design out of it so it semiresembles regular prose here. Some of the design decisions feel silly to me now, and besides, a different page size equals a different design, equals a different meaning, which requires redesign and rewrite, so I've revised them out and added new material, such as this continuing and perhaps risking-obnoxiousness sidebar.\

So technology has created this space, a kind of vacuum that waits to be filled.

I am trying to fill it up with words, with words that make some kind of meaning.

I am trying to make this mean something to you, more than just the physical act of its creation, all these words being clicked out by my keyboard through electrical impulse to the screen.

You get to watch me shuck and jive.

I am putting the *me* back in *memoir* here for you. Not that I think of *Neck Deep and Other Predicaments* or this exactly as a memoir, but it is tied up (abattoired?) in memoir, as all writing is, in memory and starlight light and the chain links of our pasts.

Think this as performance, then, and not just my normal tendency to wrap myself up in myself. I remember first hearing the word *solipsism* in college, others applying it to my work on occasion—as a critique, probably, but I never understood the problem with being solipsistic. It seemed good—to make and inhabit a world, though perhaps hermetic and overly heady—and it sounded kind of sciency and nasty in the way that literary criticism has tried to bring other disciplines to bear on literature as if they were engineers applying new technologies to a particularly tricky mining problem.

I am taking advantage (sort of—note the dearth of multimedia crap on this page, no JavaScript kicking ass, no techy trickeration taking place[†]) of the possibilities of the software. It allows me to generate more words, these worlds, and to try to metabolize the ways in which writing has meant in the past.

I type everything (and I type *everything*, now twice), though I have a set of journals, steno books mostly, not a Moleskine or whatever, that I use when I can't have my laptop in my lap warming me like a cat. Occasionally I'll start something longhand in a steno pad (I love the steno pad, that quick-flip technology designed for shorthand transcription) and try to work it out on the page before transferring it to Word or InDesign or Dreamweaver. And the work changes, almost immediately. It's really weird to watch if you watch closely.

What if I was writing everything in InDesign, which lets you do a pile of amazing effects with type on the page, on a path, curlicuing along a vector curve? And at the same time, what is lost in this, in the technology that, in trying to make things easier, reduces your options? It's not that you can't do it, but the software doesn't anticipate it, doesn't encourage that sort of play, that particular kind of construction or creative impulse. Which is probably mostly fine. I mean, how much has the ideogram or concrete poetry really done for the world? I like Apollinaire as much as the next guy, but when it comes down to it I like my horizontal lines of text, running left to right (not *boustrophedon*, as the ox plows, back and forth) across the page and beginning again at the left margin, a kind of magic—these rules are complicated enough when it comes to language, to the way I think of writing. And most people appear to agree with this—we mostly like our poetry straight, at least the we of us who like poetry at all.

See the Word autocorrect and what it does to the first letters of lines in my poems when I try to work on it; just try to write a line and then write the next at a ten degree angle up, radiating from the center of the page.

I suspect I am always going to be revisiting this question, re-solving (if not resolving) this problem. As a plus, since it's on the web, it is ephemeral— I can wipe this out at a later date and there will be no record of it here (aside from the ghostly trails in Google or websites that archive all old sites, the secret memory caches of the world). Except with you, if you got here at all, if you got this far into the netherworld. Which makes this a bit of a risk, but not the usual risk associated with publishing, committing one's words to five thousand (if you're lucky) paperback copies forever.

And actually I get excited about magic like this, divergence, not just the left-to-right repeated motion, hence these annotations are irresistible; each plowed furrow can be split, redirected, added onto, edited, worried, and continually rethought.

I'm not sure what this says about me.

Thus far, eleven out of twenty-four paragraphs in the essay start with I. It is nonfiction. It is about the world, but the world reflected slash refracted in the lens. It is about the past tense and present tense, and maybe the future tense.

I've come a long way to here. And there's much left to do.

So, for now—for the now that is captured, frozen here, somewhere between me and you—enjoy.[4]

———

1. Even this endnote on the title is an apparent lifeline out from solipsism: a mark for you to follow to the end, if you're a reader who likes to do these things, who follows orders well, and a kind of hand-hold from one part of the text to another. The footnote makes the title somehow seem less alone to me.

2. Many of us learned to type on typewriters, with two spaces after each period or terminal punctuation mark. With the advent of typing on computers, which mostly use proportional-space fonts (`fixed-width fonts, like Courier, use the same amount of space for an i as they do for an m, which is obviously much wider. So sentences tended to look more spread out, and were not as easy to read. As such, we were told to use two spaces between sentences so the sentence breaks would be more obvious`), this no longer means anything. Proportional fonts like this one, Minion Pro, are better formatted for ease of reading, and as such one should only use one space between sentences. Anything more makes the text block look loose. Write this down. Commit it to memory, if your muscle memory (all those accumulated hours of typing with the space-space after periods amount to a lot of habit, so it will be tough to break, like an addiction) allows it. And this is a minor point to be sure, but important in typographical terms, the terms that allow the construction of language on the page, and these tiny points are still sharp, are still worth considering in the technology that guides, supports our art.

3. A note on the technology of this work's composition: composed initially, as is implied, for the *Neck Deep* website, and composed (or "written," whatever that word exactly suggests at this point in time) in Macromedia Dreamweaver (and finally edited now for the page in Word, soon to be transformed through Quark or InDesign for the journal's layout), transposing the thought process of this essay from screen to page requires a lot of rethinking. I wonder if the essay changes meaning because several of its ideas are rendered impotent by virtue of this fixing of toner or ink to page, the tying down of this language to this single, definitive iteration. Can I no longer revise it for the website since it has been "published"? Which is the definitive "publication"? Does the devotion of more physical resources to the production of the artifact make it more valid or less? At the least it offers another layer of meaning and transformation to consider, which is fun. Still, check out the website for more on this—and maybe this will even have undergone another transformation or revision back to the website by the time it is printed, thus rendering it gloriously, flagrantly, interestingly obsolete.

4. So the best thing about this essay—and the website containing it that functions as its own venue for publication, which has both good and bad qualities—is that after being composed and published here (strand one), it was picked up by this great newish magazine the *Pinch,* being a cool magazine, formerly *River City,* out of the University of Memphis. They did a great print version of it (strand two) with some serious design elements that make for a very interesting and provocative read. And later, I find out today (04.16.08) that it will be reprinted in *The Best American Essays 2008,* being strand three of the same essay. Or perhaps *strand* is wrong. Instead: *strain,* something viral and expanding. All of this brings up a number of interesting questions: one is how the design elements of the piece will be translated to the *BAE* format, and how much say I will get in the process. If design means, and in this essay it certainly does, then modifying the design means meaning changes. So I would hope that I will get to tinker.

I expect, realistically, that I will not, since *The Best American Essays,* and all the books in the *Best American* series, are monuments to the canon. *BAE* is likely the most venerable-seeming, if not the most venerable (that honor goes to *The Best American Short Stories,* published continually since 1915) of the *BA* series. It is the second oldest, dating back to 1986. Which makes it a bastion of conservatism . . . until, it would appear, *now.* The conservative editorial approach is twinned with the conservative design. When the guest editor—Garrison Keillor, no less!—picked one of Diane Schoemperlen's stories for the BASS (1998, I think) it was shocking because the story included images (a first

A different *today* than elsewhere iterated in the essay, so the essay begins to incorporate a number of *now*s, a number of literary present tenses, and it's getting all wackily dimensional; I thought, additionally, of setting this sub-endnote in a tinier font than the endnotes, but there are limits to the human ability to endure design and wankery, and the printing process also has its limits.

(Well, this claim is a little bogus, approaching unjustified polemic. A Michael Martone's "Contributor's Notes" appeared a year or two ago, as did a nice piece by Robert Polito. David Foster Wallace (there he

So when I get the galleys of *BAE,* after asking to be part of the design process, and anticipating the crack design is again, like an insect or an evil genius, and maybe both) wedged his way in at least once, so that's something, too. But I definitely haven't seen anything typographically challenging, or anything approaching a complex design. Maybe this year, though, will suggest a shift in the focus of the series? Maybe this essay is a token nod to the Internet and the demise of the *Best American* tower?)

To enjoy the essay properly, especially if you're a nerd-completist who is overdramatic and obsessive, you'll want to track down all three strands of it.

in this series as far as I know). The font remains the same. The leading remains the same. The template is straightforward, reliable: it connotes authority and stability. The color changes. The guest editor changes. But that's about it.

Admittedly *BAE* doesn't include a favorite bit of *BASS,* being the excellent contributors' notes, often more interesting than the stories themselves, often including the stories' germination or the number of times the story got rejected before being at last accepted and now semi-canonized, which is a feel-good moment for all of us. The contributors' notes in *BAE* are limited to biographical information. Nothing fancy. Nothing freaky. No good stories. No sexy germination. The essays are stolid, solid, sold, they sell themselves. They don't need the *Behind the Music* version to deck them out.

"Solipsism" is also such a weird essay to see in print because it was written for this space, to be revised in perpetuity if necessary, annotated and continually maxed out with footnotes and apparatus, not for publication. Not to mention that it can now reference itself, which is appropriate, which makes it recursive and thinky if not completely dorky. And if the *BAE* contains an essay made for flux and flex, it will freeze it in some readers' minds if not my own. So I will have to break it off, this version of my solipsism, this tributary, from the essay that expands here as I type sentence after sentence into Dreamweaver, which renders it as code, not as text, as if text isn't code for something else, an Invisalign brace scaffolding over it or propping it up so it can achieve a pleasing structure.

Which is more important, I am asking myself, the generated text or the process of generating it? The action of worry-

team of Houghton Mifflin to enshrine me in the design of *BAE,* thus knighting me with typography, I find that they have simply reproduced the PDF from the *Pinch,* which is disheartening. On the upside, it forefronts the editorial mission of the series to simply reproduce the essay as-is and not change it (as changing the design would obviously change the essay); however, it's also a colossal wasted opportunity. I feel robbed, somehow, like I felt robbed when I went back to the University of Alabama to do a reading (which comes with the Book Arts program doing a great broadside for you—the same thing I did for a number of writers) only to get kind of a boring, lame broadside (sorry, designer, but it's true). Same thing with the reading I did as part of the student MFA reading series at UA, which I always designed broadsides for. I asked a friend to do the broadside since for once I didn't want the responsibility and/or pleasure of doing my own (I didn't want to have to play the role of author and designer, because for me then they were not conflated), and she made one but it, too, was a disappointment. Or maybe *robbed* isn't the word, but I feel like I've lost an opportunity for iterating a new meaning, for gaining a new shell of textual or typographical armor, for becoming someone new.

ing away at something or the remaining
chewed-up stump that once was a pen?

So strand one, my ongoing thinking on
the subject, continues to expand on my
website. Maybe the wayback machine
can locate its earlier iteration for you
if you like (check archive.org, I believe,
for it). So this becomes strand four,
while still retaining its interest in text,
in strings of words pushing out into
data space.

Out, always *out:* My penchant is for opening,
not closing, sentences (and parentheses—
and em dashes, so that this I can spawn
or take on other Is, to expand toward
the size of the big starry X that is
whatever is coming after this,
but not have to reduce back
to the previous state, to
vanish back into its
once and former
singularity . . .

I believe (though it is hard to corroborate) I was born in Ann Arbor, Michigan, on April 9, 1975, though I edited my Wikipedia page to say otherwise. I don't know much about my birth, and have no inclination to find out more. It was of note for my family, surely, since I have a lovely and breakable commemorative plate to demonstrate this. My brother has one, too, though the birth date it lists for him is a day off, the labor bleeding into the next day, so the object irritates him, rightly. It commemorates, for him, a falsity, an omission, an error, another accidental day in the womb. I don't know what the story there is and have to speculate. Who were these plates meant for? Our parents? Ourselves? The adoring public? My plate is by now only memento, but a powerful one. I don't want to donate it to Goodwill, to give someone else that thing. Nor do I want to use it (it's china!, and how odd to force visitors to eat off a plate celebrating my birth), nor can I just throw it away, inexplicably. I secretly fear[t] that if I threw it out or broke it I might cease to exist.

CEREMONY

Procession

3:06 pm, Tuesday afternoon, January 2, 2007. Former president Gerald R. Ford's remains have landed in Grand Rapids, at the airport bearing his name, and I am in position on a bridge overlooking I-196, one of the expressways cutting east to west across the bottom half of Michigan. There are already sixty people lined up on this or the next overpass east of here. We are waiting for the motorcade, which the police officer tells me is running late.

It is light outside. Tuesday afternoon. Bright and clear. A good day for ceremony.

According to one of the many press releases, "The remains will depart the museum[†] with ceremony and proceed to Grace Episcopal Church for a private funeral service." The remains will arrive at the church with ceremony, and will depart the church with ceremony.

Two University of Michigan songs will be played as part of the arrival ceremony: "Hail to the Victors" and "The Yellow and Blue." Most people know the first one from television, though probably not the second. Ford played football for the University of Michigan; his number was ceremonially retired. This music is meaningful and specific, and was selected in advance by Ford himself for the various ceremonies. The funeral and interment services, arrivals, and departures will be soundtracked by a preponderance of Bach and a number of traditional hymns, most of which I recognize.

I return to my car for warmth and music. I sit here on this strange-weathered day contemplating Gerald R. Ford, who is referred to almost exclusively with the full name and the *R*. I listen to pop music on the factory-installed stereo in my Subaru, specifically, "Ceremony" by the British band New Order. I am here along with these other thousands gathering to "line the streets" as the television stations' websites exhort us to do, in honor of Ford's remains' return to their childhood home. Can remains be said to have a childhood home? Our culture certainly thinks so. Place† of burial is important. It accrues meaning. Ford had asked to be interred here, in the crypt on the Ford museum grounds that has been waiting for him ever since I moved back to Michigan four years ago.

Ford is one of two important Fords in Michigan.

Now the crowd has doubled. They are waiting. I am waiting. I am waiting for them and for the motorcade, for the ceremony of it, the pomp and circumstance. Many people are dressed up for this. Black is appropriate, goth-appropriate, funeral-appropriate, though I'm not wearing it.

"Ceremony" is almost certainly one of New Order's best songs. I say *almost* because it's an iffy choice since it was recorded for their first album, *Movement* (1981), their first as New Order after they ceased being Joy Division after their former lead singer Ian Curtis's suicide. It was actually penned by the band as Joy Division, but never recorded past the demo stage. Bernard Sumner, who assumed singing duties in New Order, sounds a lot like he's channeling Ian Curtis on this track. It is in many ways a transitional song for them, and is arguably not a New Order song proper. The band reportedly had agreed to split if one of them left the band, so they reformed as another band, the sort of martially named electronic pop outfit New Order.

I don't know what Curtis's funeral was like, if he had one, or what.

What I wish is that I had brought my vintage Ford election campaign sign so I could hold it over my head like John Cusack does the boom box in the film *Say Anything*, an act that has become a kind of ceremony, a recognizable gesture, repeated I'm sure by tens of thousands of wooing boys. It is even iterated on an episode of *South Park*. See the boys queue outside your bedroom window, boom boxes directed up like satellite dishes to your cold, cold heart.

"Temptation," another New Order song, and the song that I'd argue is the best pop song of the last twenty-five years, and probably the best pop song ever written, plays on the car stereo.

A Ford pulls up to the curb in front of me.

The police officer conducting crowd control for this event has informed me we are not allowed to be on the side of the interstate approaching us; we are not allowed to be above Ford's body as it comes. We cannot darken the path with our shadows, if there was sun to be had here at all.

The light is bleakening now, white and weak and obscured by clouds, filtering through only intermittently. It feels appropriate, as if the weather is complying with the collective mood. If there won't be snow, it will look like there could be snow. Dead puffs of leaves line trees, a little, and the cloud cover looks threatening behind it.

Here's a douchebag in a Chevy pulling in. Those sunglasses are hard to take seriously. Come on, man.

*

World in Motion

According to the local news channel WOOD TV8's website,[†] "During the interment service, a 21-aircraft flyover in a 'missing man' formation will fly south to [N]orth[†] up the Grand River." This is a sentence taken exactly from a press release (a kind of ceremonial offering to the public that describes the various rites that will be performed as part of the national, state, and private ceremonies), "Public Participation in Michigan for State Funeral Ceremonies for President Gerald R. Ford" by JTF-NCR Public Affairs. This document describes our role.

Missing man formations became standard practice in the British Royal Air Force in World War I to demonstrate upon return how many planes returned from a mission.

Charles Schulz, the creator of the comic strip *Peanuts* got a flyby at his funeral, possibly in tribute to his use of Snoopy and the Red Baron. By

British World War II–era fighter planes, no less. Daniel Ford (no relation to any of the obvious Fords), author of *Flying Tigers: Claire Chennault and His American Volunteers, 1941–1942*, has an interesting article on the missing man formation in which he traces the history of official flybys at various funerals and important events.

The last time I saw any kind of formation of jets live was at a University of Alabama Crimson Tide football game in 2002 or 2001. The game of football, and the Alabama brand of it in particular, generates a lot of ceremony. There are fight songs ("We're gonna beat the hell outta you . . . Rammer jammer yellowhammer, Give 'em hell, Alabama"). The various processions of the home team with their bands and phalanxes of cheerleaders, dancers, and backers proceed to the stadium. There are the mascots, the drum corps. The *College GameDay* show on ESPN with the donning of the mascot's heads. The gathering of thousands upon thousands to line the streets for the progression of the glorious teams. The marching bands, remainders of a martial culture. Various military people were present at this game in a tribute to I don't remember what. Probably the war in Iraq, iteration one or two. The fighter jets flew over during "The Star-Spangled Banner." It was a totally exhilarating surprise. That's what it's for.

Ford prearranged all of this. He reportedly "kept it simple" compared to other presidential funerals. He knew of course that he would die, and made arrangements for everything, choosing the songs to be played, the pallbearers, and even asked President Jimmy Carter to speak at his funeral if he died first (and that he would return the favor if Carter died first). All (or most, anyway) of this aggregated ceremony is designed for us, not for him, by him. It is a last offering to the public.

*

In a Lonely Place

Today is a national day of mourning, an official day off for many. What can this man, this name, this president, or possibly the presidency, mean to the public, so that we should spend a day considering his life and legacy? What does it mean to Grand Rapids that the president is *from here*? He is a hero, a local. They would like to claim him as their own. I am not one of them, one of the West Michiganders (or Michiganians, if you prefer—there is some discussion about which nomenclature is preferred), but I am *from* this state where Ford's body will soon be laid to rest. Meaning I was born here, have lived the majority of my life within its perimeters, within its Great Lake embrace.

The interstate traffic will be entirely stopped from 3:00 to 4:30 pm going west toward downtown Grand Rapids. There are cars still coming through as we wait. Two cars pull over to try to get a good view of the proceedings and are immediately shooed by the police, lights and all. The flow starts to dwindle. I could call it a trickle and recognize this for the cliché that it is. Clichés are a kind of ceremony, I think, well-worn ruts, smooth stones, sayings that we like to say because they reassure us, communicate a popular idea over and over, so much so that its meaning begins to fade. Pop music is filled with clichés: it is not about lyrical invention inasmuch as it is about the hook, the bit that plays on radio, that can be repurposed now to play on cell phones as ringtones, announcing your musical taste[†] to the world. Some pop songs in the new millennium (think the Black Eyed Peas, for instance, their music repurposed to fit commercials for the NBA finals in 2002) sound a lot like jingles, themes, ringtones with some added breaks, though I don't mean this as critique. It is evolution: music is now being written for this new technology, and of course it is structured differently.

We could hear jets a couple of hours ago. Clearly a squadron of something. A bunch of jets flying pretty low. They sounded like fighters, maybe preparing for the missing man.

A guy wanders onto his porch with gut, sandwich, and drink. He is here to tailgate Ford's motorcade, a collision of two different ceremonial occasions. Both are broadcast on TV; both are a public spectacle. He is getting it partly right. He is maybe here to observe or be part of the crowd gathering outside his house.

It's good that I left my Ford campaign sign at home. I don't want to appear irreverent in this crowd, though I mostly am. I don't have any personal feelings about Ford. He is a President, and that deserves something, capitalization and the permanent present tense until death, for instance, and the state funeral, and media coverage, and so forth. I don't want to appear irreverent toward Ford in what he considers his hometown, however, for the sake of the family, for the sake of the public here slowly gathering to line the streets. Only an asshole shows up to mock or be ironic about the dead in a moment like this.

The Christmas trees are coming down, that opportunity for ceremony over. They're still set out with the trash, reminders of the recent holiday.

My brother and his wife are expecting their first child in April. They are actively developing traditions that they can pass on: it's more obvious this year than last, and I respect this, this forward thinking. They are adapting their parents' ceremonies and adding things of their own. This is the way ceremony is passed down when not writ in Bible or law, or helpfully on the Internet. My wife and I didn't do much to officially celebrate this Christmas. We had a tree and lights and presents. We drank absinthe (her present), listened to *The Goth Box* (also a present for her), newly released by Rhino, played Boggle. Watched a Christmas (horror) movie (*Black Christmas*, the original version, not the shitty 2006 remake). Ate a huge dinner. Ate leftovers. Regretted it a little. I suppose if we had a child we might need to make more of an effort to create an experience for said child to remember and dread or look forward to each year seemingly forever.

*

Fine Time

(The following italicized text is taken from a *Saturday Night Live* broadcast in 1996 with Dana Carvey playing Tom Brokaw: look it up on YouTube.com if you like since it's a lot funnier in performance than it is in script.)

> *Gerald Ford dead today at the age of 83.*
> *Gerald Ford dead today at age 84.*
> *Gerald Ford shot dead today at age 83.*
> *Gerald Ford shot dead today at the senseless age of 83.*
> *Gerald Ford senselessly shot dead at the age of 83.*
> *Gerald Ford dead today after jumping out of an office building senselessly.*
> *Gerald Ford dead today from an overdose of crack cocaine.*

Stunning news from Michigan as former president Gerald Ford was chopped into little bits by the propeller of a commuter plane.

Tragedy today as former President Gerald Ford was eaten by wolves. He was delicious.

Stunning news from Yorba Linda today as Richard Nixon's corpse climbed out of its grave and strangled Gerald Ford to death.

Gerald Ford was mauled senselessly by a circus lion in a convenience store.

Gerald Ford is dead today and I'm gay.

—

I remember watching this sketch from *Saturday Night Live*, and finding it very odd. Why Ford? I wondered. Who cared about Ford? Why foretell *his* death in particular? Mostly the bit is a send-up of Brokaw, projected onto Ford, a somewhat blank and serious midwestern face. It's hard to say why it continues to resonate, why the idea of a former president's then-future death was entertaining, or why anything stays with us in the incomprehensible matrix of memory,[†] but somehow this remains, and remains entertaining, and is now pertinent once more. You can watch it on YouTube.com if it has not been removed by the time this essay is published. Watch it in collision with the Ford funeral footage, which is probably not exciting enough to have been reposted to YouTube, though you can buy a four-DVD set of the news coverage.

And now Ford is actually dead. His crypt had been waiting for the last several years on the grounds of the Gerald R. Ford Presidential Museum in Grand Rapids, yawning (or so I imagine, projecting the human onto the world), awaiting the body. After the death of Reagan and the surprising amount of emotion and ceremony surrounding that, I have been waiting for Ford to go (it is weird to say, but true) until this week, when it occurred. Potential energy, now kinetic.

And now Dana Carvey, like Gerald Ford, has passed into a kind of oblivion, if not yet physical cessation. His own website, danacarvey.net, was last updated in 2005. Maybe he will return at death, have a well-attended, broadcast funeral procession. Really, I feel closer to him, have more memories of him stored in my brain, than I do to former president Gerald R.

Ford. He entertained, even haunted me. He is best associated with his impression of the first Bush president, probably, or the Church Lady bit. And as those characters have ceased to matter, so has he.

Dana Carvey, dead at 84, forgotten by the public until this very moment. He will be remembered for his bit on Gerald Ford: at least one of them is dead from an overdose of crack cocaine.

Dana Carvey passed away today, passé no more at last.

Dana Carvey, dead at 83, devoured by wolves.

⋆

Vanishing Point

There are far more people now in the street ahead. It will be a serious crowd. I will join them and brave the cold, a statement in itself of my support for them, for the city, for the State, for its capital S and flags. There will be many of us citizens out here. The media will be out in force. Hundreds of thousands are coming into the city to pay their respects. It is more than a little strange, a kind of tourism, maybe.

This anticipation is somehow festive. A crowd of about 150 is on the south side of Eastern Street NE waiting for the president's body. Probably twenty kids are in attendance, and they yell periodically: "Is he coming?" "Is that him?" "He's coming!" and so on. They could be talking about Santa, Jesus, Justin Timberlake. A man is there with a large flag that he unfurls and waves. It is surprisingly emotional, at least a little bit. Like the others in attendance, I am not sure how to respond. A woman next to me asks if we should cheer or applaud. Yet when the motorcade comes— thirty to forty cars—there is only silence, the sound of wind, of thinking, of memory.

My crowd, the growing *us* of this experience, is diverse. A lot of parents with their kids, eager for some kind of celebration. Our bodies are adjacent to each other; we share pheromones. It could be a parade, almost, if not for the cops and the photographers and television cameras. I'm sure there is a specified order as to who comes first in these things—it always has the appearance of order, which is what ritual, ceremony is all about. Ford's casket comes fourth. Maybe fifth. Probably the number is symbolic. He, or what remains of he, is followed by a phalanx of American-made cars: Lincolns, Chevys, and—yes—Fords.

The public is invited via press release to queue to see the body. Ford is now seven days[†] dead but still on display.

⋆

This Time of Night

8 pm. I am finished baking bread and two friends and I go down to queue for the viewing of the body in repose. We park and go down only to find out that the wait time is seven hours. Thousands are lined up down here, curlicuing around corners and blocks. Neil Diamond is in the air since the queue starts next to Rosa Parks Circle, where teenagers are skating on artificial[†] ice. It hasn't been below freezing for a week or so, though it's cold enough to make this more of an ordeal than it probably needs to be.

Seven hours? For *this* president?

We turn around. My backup plan is to come back at 2 am when the line must surely be more reasonable.

1:15 am. My friend Charlie and I go back in his large Japanese-made SUV and join the line. We get to sit inside. There are still at least three thousand people here surrounding us. The old are here. The very young are here. A lot of high school–age kids. There are tents. Sixty plus lines snaking back and forth in the huge convention center. At least it's warm enough inside. The collective energy of our thousands of bodies, all that breath and body heat collected, is something to feel. It is a little bit electric, exciting. No one has an official time on the wait, but we wait for close to two hours, and make it about a third of the way. I feel it is decision time. Charlie's willing to go for it, but it will be an all-night experience, and he proposes an early breakfast if we can find a place that's open. I see a handful of my students, people I have passed on the street. Some of them were probably in the crowd along the interstate with me before.

It turns out that I do not care enough to hold the line all night, lacking the proper reverence or motivation. At the halfway point, at my behest, we check out. I wonder what it would mean for me to stand in line for six hours to make it through to stand in the same room as the flag-draped closed coffin. My left foot has been aching badly for the last several days, and standing for this time has not improved it. Who stands all night to be in the same room with the body of the former president just for a moment before being ushered through?

No cell phones were officially allowed. Nor were cameras, though many had their cell phones anyhow. The idea was to preserve a kind of silence, probably, or to make it impossible for people to snap pictures?

In the next days I talk with a couple of dozen people who stayed in line, who got into the inner sanctum, had their minute or two with the flag-draped coffin, signed the official guest book,[†] got their names inscribed in history. Of course the coffin isn't open, so there is a barrier between the world and the body, not to mention the whole thing is roped off, and security is everywhere so as to enforce order, decorum. So they waited to pay their respects.

*

State of the Nation

Back to the procession. A set of kids are snacking on a bag of Doritos as we watch the motorcade. They treat this like a parade, sans music and candy. The television news commentators tell us that we are all becoming a part of history. Is that our motivation, to be one with history? Or is it an outpouring of support for the hometown boy turned president? Or a show of confidence in what Ford represents to the culture, meaning (with air quotes) "Midwestern Values" like hard work and honesty and unpretentiousness? Are the crowds gathering to make a statement to the contrary of the current red-state/blue-state culture? Is the caption for this photograph *We Are In Fact One?*

It's strange to be part of a crowd here in reverence of a dead president. It is unsettling to be standing in a crowd at all, physically part of an obvious *us*, in proximity, and probably in solidarity by default. In my lifetime I have disapproved of most of our presidents, and have not had much reverence for them. I don't listen to country, kick ass for the Lord, or support the war. My family has few connections to the military, though we spent several years in Saudi Arabia, where my dad worked for the government, and we spent significant time on a military compound that would be hit by a Scud missile a few years after we had left. He did not go to war. Went to grad school, quite probably with the intention of avoiding the draft. He and my mother[†] joined the Peace Corps after. We are a crowd of recent academics. While I have a friend in the service, I don't think about the idea of serving one's country in this way much, if at all, except to think about how strange it is, and to be thankful for others' observation of this duty, at least in the abstract. I know something about that culture, and the world beyond this country. I watch the coverage of the wars on television.

*

Regret

A week after Ford's remains have been finally and permanently interred, and several days after the media coverage has subsided in favor of something more exciting and less reverent, I am at the bar where I sing karaoke[†] some Friday nights. A woman dedicates the Bette Midler song "Wind Beneath My Wings" to her son, who's coming home in a couple of weeks from Iraq, whom everyone in the bar seems to know well. There are cheers. My instinct is to laugh, but I cannot. I feel embarrassed not to have anyone close to me who is serving in this way. It's easy to distance myself from these ideas, this part of our culture, of our culture's martial interactions with other cultures, all the procedures designed to corral the edge of the inhabited world into the impression of solidity. I can laugh it off. I can be irreverent. This irreverence implies a kind of recognition, though, that the subject at hand does have some potential gravity that I have no access to. I can have my ironic moment listening to this performance: I can hold myself above the crowd here at The Point, on Grand Rapids' more blue-collar west side—and the crowd is totally into it, not examining but enjoying it, as it should be, as we should be, since karaoke[†] is a participation in a culture, both the culture that produced the song being sung and the culture that is listening to the (often not very good) performances of the song. If I am a good citizen of karaoke, I need to get behind her. Part of you can sit back and remark how everybody (but you, but us, as this implies) sucks, or how good they are, but part of you—again, if you are a good citizen of karaoke country, if you live by its Bill of Rights, its constitution, its random set of bylaws (no jumping the rotation, no booing the singers, no matter how bad, though maybe if they're unenthusiastic it's acceptable: if they're not buying into the culture, the culture does not need to buy into them)—must endorse it. Your presence endorses it. By virtue of your ass being in the chair, and your hand probably lifting a drink to your open mouth, you're there, and that counts for something. So I applaud. And she is good, and her son will, I think, be proud, as she is proud of him.

I think you should sing periodically, too, though I don't think this is the rule. If you are an enthusiastic member of the audience, you are doing your part here as a citizen, but still It Is Good to participate more actively. It's like you're running for public office, not just voting, though you're likely to lose, and that losing is part of the experience, a civic lesson, a contribution. Losing, you fall backward into a network of other arms—if this isn't making too much of this—and are conveyed back to the stage for your encore.

I do sing, though my instinct is to do Erasure, or Cher, or something celebratory and provocative in straight bars like this. My first song flops totally, though for the life of me (a weird cliché, again, that familiar stone in the hand, designed to increase the gravity of the statement, suggesting that if it were worth my life even then I could not possibly remember) I can't remember what I sang now when trying to revisit this experience. This is even weirder that I can't remember, can't recover the memory of not being rewarded or appreciated.

The second one is a more considered choice: you can't go wrong with "Every Rose Has Its Thorn" (which I have gloriously performed at an open mic in college, culminating with me smashing my guitar on the stage and storming off—the closest I got to my rock moment, my preaching from the pulpit, my place on the ballot, really), and it goes well, though the guy in the rotation just in front of me does another Poison song, "Something to Believe In," which is more ponderous, is Later, post-awesome Poison, but to his credit, it is a much less obvious choice, and I am suddenly self-conscious about my own decision. Is it too easy? I wonder. Too open for camp? As the intro starts up the crowd is suddenly entirely with me: we are, no doubt, an us, and it is fabulous. I am part of something. I tell CC to take it to the bridge, and at least I think the crowd cheers. Last week I did Billy Idol's "Dancing with Myself" (song #2, chronologically, on my best pop songs compilation) and that went over well, as it should, a song about our essential (maybe even existential) aloneness and working through it. When we sing these songs we are one with Billy Idol, with the soul of pop, with the populace. Regardless of our inability to perform them adequately, our participation is important. Buying the records and making mix[t] tapes in high school for girls we totally loved was important, and remains important. Ranking songs and making exhaustively researched lists is important, both to my participation in the culture (teenage geek boy) and to my demonstration of knowledge of and in this culture, my acknowledgment of the importance of pop.

This is my civic participation, and as I do it, my little shell of irony recedes. It will go back up later, certainly, but for now I am subsumed in something new for me.

Even the guy who insists on doing the same songs every Friday night (The Beastie Boys' "Fight for Your Right to Party" with added swears, Puddle of Mudd's "She Fuckin' Hates Me," also with added swears, so that when I look it up online I find out the title is in fact an underwhelming "She Hates Me"), and not all that well, but with great enthusiasm: he pats me on the back later, introduces himself. He is a genial guy. We are men here. Possibly we will play some pool.

All of this is unexpectedly moving.

*

Round & Round

Ceremony *is* order, arbitrary, evolving, but not too quickly, stilled by the call to history, to stricture, to authority. I have applied an artificial order to this essay, parceling this story into unrelated moments, titling each section after songs by New Order (an easter egg for music geeks, and now you get your invitation into the club), creating a kind of new order, a momentary rigidity, an exoskeleton through which fact or thought can move and become a citizenry, a sudden we.

*

Dreams Never End

"The Gerald Ford Funeral Video Compilation features the arrival ceremony at St. Margaret's Episcopal Church in Palm Desert, CA, official ceremonies in Washington, DC, services in Grand Rapids, Michigan, and final interment at the Gerald Ford Presidential Museum. Official events in Washington include the arrival at Andrews Air Force Base, the funeral motorcade to the Capitol, official funeral services in the Capitol Rotunda and the National Cathedral. This video set is available on four DVDs or five VHS tapes."

*

Everyone Everywhere

"Nearly 50,000 people signed the Condolence Books on the grounds of the Gerald R. Ford Presidential Museum in Grand Rapids and Library in Ann Arbor beginning at 1:30 am on Wednesday, December 27, 2006, through 5:00 pm Thursday, January 4, 2007.

"An estimated 36,000 visited the U.S. Capital [*sic*] Rotunda as President Ford lay in State.

"As President Ford lay in repose at the Museum, Tuesday afternoon through Wednesday morning, some 62,000 people paid their respects, including the estimated 57,000 people who entered the queue through DeVos Place and waited patiently in line.

"In addition, an estimated 75,000 people lined the streets of Grand Rapids to welcome President Ford home on January 2, 2007 and during the funeral services on January 3, 2007.

"Pallbearers for the services in Grand Rapids, MI: Martin J. Allen, Jr., Mary Sue Coleman, Richard M. DeVos, Richard A. Ford, David G. Frey, Pepi Gramshammer, Robert L. Hooker, Frederick H. G. Meijer, Jack Nicklaus, Leon W. Parma, Glenn 'Bo' Schembechler (In Memoriam), Peter F. Secchia, L. William Seidman, and Steve Van Andel."

Some of these people—most even—are honorary pallbearers (at least one was dead at the time). They did not physically bear the pall, the cloth spread over the coffin, hearse, or tomb. It is a ceremonial designation.

INTERIORITY

The most popular color in the section of the Ball[†] that I have in my possession is brown. At the center of what looks to me to be fifty layers of paint, the center is a yellow splotch surrounded by a spread of white. It looks like an egg. This is not, of course, the center of the Ball, but an illusion brought to you by slicing a section off an approximated sphere that will create its own impression of a ball with a center, necessarily, and layers spreading out inside it. It is almost indescribable. You should see it. The layers are irregular, increasingly. It is important that you can take home a tiny slice of the Ball. Mike and Glenda understand this, our desire to be part of something, to populate a country, an idea, an ideology, a desire to count for something, a desire to not and never vanish. To center, to occupy the center. The geographic center of the fifty states is in South Dakota, and the center of the forty-eight continental states is in Kansas.

The only reason you can buy a Ball shaving is because of gravity. The paint on each layer drips down slightly to the bottom of the Ball, so the Ball elongates slowly toward the ground. This effect is exaggerated as the Ball becomes larger. Because of this the Carmichaels have to shave off the bottom sections periodically in order to keep its ball shape. If you visit the Ball, these slices are available to take home for a donation.

There are at least twelve towns named "Center," hopefully longing to be part of something larger than themselves. The majority of them are in the

Middle West (Colorado, Indiana, Indiana—there are two!—, Kentucky, Missouri, Nebraska, North[†] Dakota, Wisconsin, Wisconsin—also two!—, Texas, and Washington). To my untrained eye I could imagine Nebraska or possibly Colorado occupying the geographic center of the United States. The center of the earth itself is solid iron, giving rise to the magnetic field. This is stuff you may remember from grade school geology, or Jules Verne's *Journey to the Center of the Earth*, which should probably have been titled *Journey to the Interior of the Earth*, as it never gets close to the center itself.

Every town wants to be part of something larger than itself. Hence the phenomenon of sister cities (or *town twinning*, as it's known in Europe). Alexandria, Indiana, however, has no sister cities. As of May 2005 (the date on which the city last produced its "Community Profile" downloadable fact sheet), its population is 6,260. Its unemployment rate (countywide anyhow) is 6.1 percent. Thus approximately as of 2005, 381 residents of Alexandria are waiting for a call. Maybe they've gotten bored and tired of trying to find work. Finding work is hard, and it has surely become harder since 2005. You might find them on their couches, or in their yards, or in their bars. It is midway between Cleveland and St. Louis. It is 865 feet above sea level. It is just a place.[†] A place like other places. Surrounded by space[†] and statistics.

Alexandria, Indiana, is also not currently seeking a sister city (according to the Sister Cities International website[†]) but Nova Veneza, Brazil, is, and Nova Veneza might be a good match for Alexandria, Indiana. Nova Veneza's population is 6,404. Its main employers are two slaughterhouses, a company that makes and installs electric lines, a candy manufacturer, and several manufacturers of corn flour. Its first choice for a sister city is someplace in the USA (second choice: Italy). Alexandria's main employers are Red Gold (tomato products), a machine and tool company, a maker of patio furniture, and a company specializing in commercial site maintenance. Both of these cities sound lonely. Nova Veneza's top two choices for sister cities? Atlanta or Nashville. Nova Veneza wants to date up. We all want to date up and out of our league, to exceed ourselves, to be acknowledged by whatever stratum is just above our own.

What is inside the Ball? Paint. What is inside what is inside the Ball? More paint. Eventually: a baseball, an idea, a dream of fields, a field of dreams. Everything can be subdivided, reduced, downward, to dreams, and then synapses firing while we sleep. The Ball can be reduced to a base-ball if all the paint were to be stripped away. The baseball's center is a sphere of cork. What is inside the idea of the Ball is something else entirely. I am not sure. The aforementioned documentarians have their theory. I'm not convinced even Mike or Glenda knows. Can we really take apart and see underneath our actions to what prompted them, what is underneath the body and its twitching, all the brain and synapse shot and glistening mystery? We all want to get inside ourselves, split the nut that is the head of someone else. That's what sentences are for.

Inside the Ball is the future. Or: Inside the Ball is—more literally—the past.

I watch television shows that feature what is inside the walls of old houses. People put a single woman's shoe inside a wall for luck, or so the television tells me. I could believe it. If the Ball can exist, electric lines and highways flexing all around it, drawing my attention, our attention, each of these sentences into a knot, warping them, bunching them as if inside a fist, then almost anything is possible. We could be anywhere thinking, thinking *anywhere*. My uncle is somewhere, dying tonight, his lungs slowly filling and shutting down. I am here, imagining it, trying to find my way to imagine it, to summon it as if via magic. I am on the very periphery of this side of my family's collective ball of life. I get updates through my brother. Instead of being there I am here and so conscious of it.

Inside the Ball must be us. It is—we are—either stupid or glorious. As the Northern chunk of the United States begins to shed itself of leaves, baring earth, coating it with color, below, the world does cool. Not the Arizona part of the world, not that much, nor the parts that are, like Arizona, like Florida, locations of constant weather and dangerous flora, fauna, anaphora: Camino Real, Camino de Palmas, Arroyo Chico, Arroyo Grande. Tucson becomes iterations of Tucson. The world spawns ideas of itself, and then spawns, itself. Media representations give life to our visions of ourselves. We see the Ball and we want to see more balls, to build more balls, to erupt into a frenzy of ball-making and endorsement. That is, if you are like me, if you can be inhabited like me by an idea of such force and genius, such ineffable, inevitable bullheadedness that it becomes indescribably excellent, then you are already starting to build and coat and recoat and recoat your own ball in your mind. I have started mine with coats of lotion all along my body. Scented oils and mineral salts for the bath. Sentences that wrap around the body. Flakes of language. Paper. Dead technologies. It resists description. It puts the lotion in the basket. It rubs the lotion on its body. I rub the lotion on my body. I put the lotion in the basket. My hands are on the Ball. I have painted it. I have applied a coat of paint. I am one of thousands. I am among the thousands on the street this early afternoon in October in Michigan being pelted by raindrops and leaf bits curling downward from deciduous trees. I am just outside the Mystery Spot, a tourist attraction (North of the gloriously underwhelming Sea Shell City) in Michigan's Upper Peninsula featuring a number of optical illusions, such as balls rolling uphill. I am outside my friend Emma's house waiting for her to emerge. I am in the very center of Grand Rapids tonight, thinking about the city's arms laid flat and stretching toward the second biggest Great Lake. I am in the coffee shop inside my headphones, inside my head, inside this sentence, every sentence, every page. I am in Ames, Iowa, eight years ago, driving Domino's into the steaming, manure-smelling summer night. I am on U.S. 30, driving a pizza to a topless[†] club where I will deliver it to a tired woman. I am that older shell of self, tired and thinking about graduate school, earning crap money working for people younger than myself, on the edge of just driving off in that car with that pizza and never returning to Ames, Iowa. I am inside the late-night occasional traffic stream and I could be anywhere. It feels like I am in the center of the country, so big is that sky above me, so evident is our importance according to the dozens of visible blinking lights, satellites, maybe, above us, or moons of anything, the occasional airplane contrail revealing another light behind it in increments. I am in that same place a week later, on the way to deliver a pizza to Story City, Iowa, which I will never make in time since it's a solid half hour away and I have no idea why my manager sent me there. I am about to be stiffed on the tip by a nine-year-old sent by his parents to give me money expressly to avoid facing the delivery driver. I am in that space, that itchy golf shirt, with that heated bag beside me, hoping to experience one of the many appealing narratives involving women answering the door naked or wearing very little, yes, very little, which will never happen, so I am amidst an evening dream and the stories we tell ourselves about our jobs in order to make them interesting, to fill them with future, with possibility. I am driving one of these nights wondering if I can leave myself here by leaving my job, my car, my clothes, my classes, my shedding skin, my self, on the edge of something that eludes me. Radio and microwave and cellular telephone towers appear on every side of me bleeding Morse to low-flying planes. Fireflies light up the field around me by the thousands and I feel held up, buoyed, cradled inside something, whether past or future, midwest grid of street and field and field and field, and I am inside something. I am Mike and Glenda inside, we are just an us who have followed an idea, a stupid idea, as far as it can seemingly go. Inside the Ball is the Midwest, is us, is suffrage, the right to vote, to count, to show up anywhere and be surrounded with love, or a simulacrum of.

My stepmother periodically suggests that I write about[†] her, that is, the part of her that she shows me and wants represented (glorified? beatified?) somehow in prose. Or even poetry would do, she says. Admittedly, there's a lot to write about. When I told her about this book she wanted to know if she was in it. My sister-in-law has also requested to show up in a book,[†] as if the most important act of love a writer can show is attention, regurgitation, the lavishing of imagination (or not) upon the person. I guess it's better to be noticed than not. My father would be much happier if I never wrote about him again. I have no clue how my brother feels. My wife would be irked to be omitted entirely or the subject of an essay. My friend Nicole's husband would prefer, I am told, to remain nameless in prose. Her book is about food. He eats the food. She cooks the food and writes about the food and her family in sentences that are as aromatic and rich as the food. But the husband would prefer to vanish, like my father, like my mother,[†] maybe. The rest would rather stand up and be counted. They assert themselves in conversation via phone and email. I don't know what I think, whether I would want to show up in others' work (probably). I would if I were praised. I love the experience of reading about a place[†] or person that I know, this being probably the attraction of tabloids for many. But it's the opposite of tabloid, the elevation of our regular lives to text. So here you go, stepmother, you are thus named: Paula. And Katie. And Erik. And Terry. And Megan. And Ben. Should I feel guilt for naming these names, for showing them off here? For not showing them off enough? For the task, like the water, is wide, and the crossing's a risk. I'll consign it to a footnote emerging from an asterisk emerging from almost nothing.

ASSEM-BLOIR†: ON SIGNIFICANCE

Most experiences as they are lived claim an importance beyond their real significance. Each new friend, new place,† new love seems spectacular at the moment of inception. In retrospect, few stand the test of time.

There is no such thing as an unnoticed event, a trivial subject. Our lives are made up mostly of an accumulation of small incidents.

Do you know what worries me most about this memoir? That I'm always the smart one. Always the one with the last word. Always the one with the heartless quip, the derisive bon mot.

There is no need, I think, to apologize for a point of view which discovers in what people read, or look at, or admire, or laugh at (or just accept!) as important a stencil of their national history as can be found in their battles or elections or their metaphysics. Nor any need, either, to pretend that there isn't a lot of just plain fun in remembering how things used to be.

I was kicking the idea around in my own head to see how it fit, but tossing it around to others as if it were an idea already set in concrete.

How should one approach the history of his own times? Finally, perhaps, it is an accumulation of small things that changes us, the unexpected and unnoticed incidents that signal moments of transition, pointing us in an entirely different direction, almost without our knowledge, often without our consent.

There is some wisdom in it. By reading and retyping thousands of lines from over a hundred memoirs I feel like I have absorbed them, consumed them, become them, stuffed them in my mouth, enveloped their shells with my own. When we say a thing, it is an incantation. When we write a thing, we are summoning. When we read a thing, we are susceptible to magic. I becomes a we, a little less lonely.

We had become beggars and we broke all the rules.
If I could write and re-write a thing I could absorb it.

Halloween. Grand Rapids again. I see a girl dressed up as an asterisk and I give her warm congratulations. My friend Nicole is dressed as Today's Mail, she tells me. She has a thing for abstract costumes. I am surrounded by twelve teenagers in impressive *Super Mario Bros* costumes (mushroom, Princess Peach, Mario, Luigi, Bowser, Toad, etc.), and a friend tells me she saw another group dressed this way, as if somehow these constumes have found their time, or descended from a social networking website[†] exhorting its members to dress up like this. This group was charming. They were excited. They looked good. Ready for the night. I was in the video game again, but this time the game was in the world. Seeing them, I felt special, though I was dressed as myself, as nothing special, having no party to attend. I was a seeing eye tonight. I was dressed as nothing at all.

GEAS

Gary Gygax is dead. Sorry. Nerds, friends, fellow travelers, I am really sorry for your loss. He has left the building. There will be, at the risk of sounding flip, no resurrection. The founder of *Dungeons & Dragons,* and in fact the whole idea of role-playing games, often blamed for our increasingly many social ills, from the destruction and desecration of our youths and their drugged-out, sexed-up high school escapades to the difficulty we increasingly have in separating game, or fiction, or film, or dream, from reality, just to name a few, Gygax found religion in the years before his death. He increasingly believed in the spirit exceeding the body, a corollary to *Dungeons & Dragons,* which allows the body to be resurrected, resuscitated, raised from the dead with a high-level spell. While the theology of *D&D* has undergone a number of overhauls (from dalliances with demons and devils, immortals, the Ethereal and Astral planes, and some really whacked-out and interesting stuff to a more traditional pantheon of deities and demigods and dragons that live forever), it has always been based on the idea that the character extends beyond the body into the nothingness or whatever you want to fill it with thereafter, at least until the night of gaming ends. When your character died, you could either make up a new one or else undertake a quest to try to get your character resurrected.

Gygax died a week ago, nearly, and the fact that I didn't hear about it until now depresses me further. To think I am so disconnected from this gaming, fantasy hinterland from whence I emanated in my teenage years is near-crushing. I do claim the moniker of *gamer,* as a descended *D&D* player, descended as in testicles, as in no longer playing, as in having abandoned that imaginative and physical life or lack thereof in college, having given it up after a decade, easily, of playing and entering into that storyspace after my mother's[†] death, maybe that being a factor, maybe that opened me up for it, and living in my dad's duplex, dice clattering across the downstairs kitchen table, the light buzzing fluorescent above us, with my brother and my friends, Chris, Matt, Jerry (whose brief dwarf character was named "Cooler"), occasionally Jody (now murdered, and putting her into the essay at all, iterating her name, almost obliges me to address that welt, that hurt, to do something with it, she who has left her body some years ago, though I did so at length in another text that will go unmentioned here), and a host of others, who joined us for a game, or for the better part of a decade.

This fact, the fact of his departure from this mortal whatever, feels like punctuation. It closes a door on my life, a door that I'd forgotten about. Deaths do that. They make a sound.

On the day I am trying to reckon with the loss of Gygax the news is made public that I am leaving this, my current job, a good job with good people, for another job, which will also presumably have good people. The body is already quavering, contemplating giving up my house, this city,[†] this skyline, this weather, and this, my native state, for something else with scorpions and desert. As I work on generating this bit of prose, faculty stop by my office to mock-accuse me for leaving, and to congratulate me. It is a mix.[†] Their emotions, mine. I have loved this office with its ravine view and humming fan amid the silence, and green technology. This essay borders on an elegy for this job, this former iteration of Monson, which will be left behind and vacated like this space,[†] like my parents' former houses, one after another, and an elegy for my students whom I have loved also in my way. But elegy is grandiose. I am becoming maudlin. It is too much. I pine, opine. I move close and I push away.

I don't even know if this is true emotion, or if it's a role I am expected to play, and am so playing, or how to tell the difference, if there is any at all. If my colleagues and friends here will be sad, exactly, to see me go, or if it is a social obligation, self-pity, envy, or what. I feel I am of this place,[†] that it has acted on me, like other formative settings in my life. In *D&D* we might call this place, a continuity of character and mythology and action, the overarching scope of the adventures, an arc, *a campaign.* Sometimes when the Dungeon Master loses his players, as in they no longer want to play, or are dissatisfied, or bored, or have had their outside lives interfere with the shared ongoing fantasy, or in a case where the plot has become too byzantine, too dumb, or the players too spoiled, too fat with loot, you have to scrap it, the whole world you've created, and start another.

You can also buy another, buy into one of the ongoing published campaign worlds. Greyhawk was one. Forgotten Realms, another. Krynn, home of the *Dragonlance* books, another. There are dozens of these created worlds with their own continuities, clashing races, dark elves and gnomes, and clans and what have you. With the Internet and the rise of online, open-source gaming, there are surely thousands of collective, published imaginations for you to choose from.

For me it comes down to not wanting to let inertia, the fact of this job and this role, this office, these classes, these students, direct my life. To not get too comfortable, if this isn't a story I am telling myself to enable motion. I haven't signed the new contract yet. I'm still hedging, just a little, until it arrives.

Perhaps it is the province of those who are self-involved, or sensitive, or inward directed, or neurotic, or solipsistic, to overanalyze at length, to ramble on and circle the fact in prose. It allows me to contain two roles at least: both excited at new prospects and sad to be leaving, and aware of these things, both existing. I can play both sides. I can feel torn. I can generate enough emotion to want to line up sentences on a page. Equivocation is one of my character flaws. I like to have it both ways, always, even. It's not quite duplicity, but it's on the road toward it. Equal and opposite reactions. The mind casts itself as passive, as watcher of the action, not as actor. I want to talk about it, and to do it, but to hold the imaginative possibility of action and inaction.

In *D&D* your character has an *alignment.* This describes her moral compass, her approach to good and evil, law and lawlessness. It can range from Lawful Good to Chaotic Evil. The alignment defines your character perhaps more than anything else. It circumscribes the way you can play your role, whether you are a weeping willow type or a man of action, whether you subscribe to the life of the mind or the body heaving the axe at a troll, and whether you are a force for good or not in this or another world.

And even as I am always reckoning, always analyzing, equivocating, I move.

I have to admit that the idea of reckoning with the loss of Gygax is a reductive one: it's naive, a lack of specificity, of deep engagement with the subject. I don't think of him that often, and I'm not even sure how to pronounce his name, which g gets the soft and which the hard, and so I vary (ending up on soft-g *gy* and hard-g *gax,* but if you use both hard g's it's more warriorish, something your paladin could shout on the battle-field as he charges toward a swarming force of orcs). For me he was as myth already, even as living man. I'm sure he got that a lot, being the honored guest at thousands of RPG conferences, having his myth tended to and honored publicly, even as the public thinks about his past and not his present, not his finding-Jesus, not his new game systems. (In 1985 he left *D&D* to TSR, his former publishing company, who owned it until it was sold to Wizards of the Coast in the late '90s; originally TSR stood for Tactical Studies Rules, demonstrating *D&D*'s origin in tactical wargames, and eventually the company jettisoned this moniker so it no longer stands for anything at all.) So the Gygax I know (or conceive of) is at least twenty years old, like light from a closer star, and just a name, almost, a reputation, a signifier that points to the emanation of this gameworld in my and others' lives. I know him not at all except by reputation, as what he means, or meant, or, well, means, still: let's be honest, his name will be yoked to *D&D* and this particular variety (if not all varieties) of nerdery for decades to come, as we see how far the effects of *D&D* and RPG and gaming culture have permeated our media, our stories.

At the same time in the last few years *D&D* has become acceptable to talk about publicly again. The actor slash action star Vin Diesel cops to it, even writing an introduction to a recent retrospective (and awful) book[†] about the game's history. Television satirist Stephen Colbert talks *D&D,* or, failing that, the work of J. R. R. Tolkien, about every week or two on his show. The musician Final Fantasy has a whole album centered around the concept of the various schools of magic in third-edition *Advanced Dungeons & Dragons.*

All these sightings of *D&D* in the public and now-slightly-less-shameful world, and in particular reading an essay, "Destroy All Monsters," by nov-

elist Paul La Farge in a recent issue of the *Believer*, means a lot to me because it enables me to come out, to admit and talk on and worry my history
with this dorky pastime, which is a way of saying a history with collab-
orative story or storytelling, which is a subgenre of *interactive fiction* as
the current academic term applies to what we formerly called "text adventures" like *Zork* and so on in the world.

Fuck. There's so much here, embedded, impacted in the subject. Like
anything suitably primal, it resists being teased apart.

Outside a dude in a black trenchcoat and ponytail walks by the window.
His tote bag features a bunch of unidentifiable pins. Though I don't know
him, his look tells me he is a fellow traveler, that he knows what dodecahe-
dron means, that he could bust out some adjustments to saving throw statistics, that he might, as I did once, subscribe to *Dragon* magazine.

About once every three years I am called to rescue or condemn a box of
artifacts from my former life (this time, those *Dragon*s) from their position
moldering in the basement or the garage. This entails evaluating, reliving,
simulating,† or reconceiving of this past life, this former Monson, or stage
thereof, and looking at it closely, reentering that space, and deciding what
to do with it, whether I can fit into those clothes or not, whether I'd want
to. These old actions are bizarre to the new me, biologically foreign (yet I
still contain traces). I can't imagine sitting in the basement of a house with
a bunch of other teenagers, surrounded by a tripartite Dungeon Master's
screen filled with statistics and probably a picture of a wizard, exploring
some imaginary dungeon.† Instead I have no problem with sitting in some
dude's rec room (or mine if I had a rec room), playing video games, exploring an imagined, virtual space for hours, not speaking, barely moving. I
cannot comprehend my former tooth-killing interest in eating powdered
sugar with a spoon directly out of the bag, occasionally inhaling some by
accident and shredding my mucous membranes, all while quaffing liters
of Mountain Dew and rubbing my little belly like a buddha. (I know the
word *quaffing* only as a result of the computer game *Larn*, a version of a
more popular computer game called *Rogue*, both of which involve wandering through dungeons rudimentarily represented as black space on the
black monochrome computer screen and lit up in accordance with your
character (itself represented by a character, an ASCII glyph, like a dollar
sign or the letter *x* or something, I don't quite remember) as it meandered
through the darkness, and turned black space into a white dot against that

space. The monsters in the game were all represented by an alphanumeric character, like a *t* for a troll and a *g* for a goblin, and your commands were entered via one-key commands from the keyboard. *Q*, then, was for *quaff*, as in quaffing a healing potion or a poison remedy. Both *Larn* and *Rogue* were single-player versions of *D&D*, albeit with almost no graphics, not much actual playing a role, and no social engagement with anything beyond the screen. But they were, in their way, beautiful and immersive.

All these selves[†]—my Atari 2600 self, recently adopted from said garage, my PC-virus-writing self, also recently recalled from my parents' garage, my teenage criminal self, my computer-gaming self—they are like characters within the larger campaign of the person, the player, being me, probably (I assume). The distance, psychologically, biologically, between there and now, between those cells, those synapse configurations and these, is almost too great to comprehend. Which should give me hope. That we can grow through obsessions like these suggests a life of disposable stages, something new ahead, a new job, a new place, new levels of dorkiness.

I'm going to head home from this office life in tribute and play that character again, sit down in my sleepy hollow chair, pop a couple of Mountain Dews, order Domino's, and bury my head for a while in video games. Maybe I'll make my saving throw against permanent depression. The Mountain Dew will give me a +4 bonus.[†]

*

"Q: How many times per day can a hellhound breathe fire?

"A: There is no limit on the total number of times that a hellhound can breathe fire, but it may only breathe when the dice roll given in the 1983 *Expert Rulebook*, page 51, says it can breathe fire." ("Sage Advice," Skip Wiliams, *Dragon* #124)

"Q: *Geas* and *quest* spells are much abused. For example, couldn't an evil magic-user *geas* a character to never attack him? Couldn't an evil cleric do a similar thing with *quest*?

"A: A *quest* must be a specific and finite task; the victim must be able to take actions that will bring about the end of the *quest*, or the spell has no effect. A *geas* is similar to a *quest* in that it must be specific." ("Sage Advice," Skip Wiliams, *Dragon* #124)

Geas is one of those words that I try to deploy periodically in conversation, or, worse, in Scrabble, where I am destined to lose by virtue of my reliance on knowledge gleaned from fantasy books, mythology, or *Dungeons & Dragons*. This happens way more often than it should because I usually can't differentiate actual knowledge from fantasy knowledge. The wall between the two is glass, and flimsy, clear. In one of my ancient Greek classes I used some bit of knowledge from the (old, crappy, fantasy) movie *Krull* to underscore a point I was making about the Cyclops, that he had traded one of his eyes to one god or another for the ability to see the future, but that he was tricked: the only future he could see was the day of his own death (or possibly the day of anyone's death, which would be a little more useful). This tidbit was met by the laughter of my Greek professor, who asked me where I got that from. Hmm. It was in my brain with all the other knowledge. What made this different?

Geas comes from *geis* in Celtic, Scottish, or Welsh mythologies, which vary a bit. It is essentially a specific curse/quest that a character must live up to or undergo. It is a spell (interchangeable with *quest*) used by magic users (wizards/sorcerers/necromancers/illusionists or any other subgenre of mage—*D&D* likes to tease these distinctions out at length), or by clerics (priests, druids, users of religious magic) in *D&D*. *Dungeons & Dragons* is an exceptionally complex and expansive system, covering, I'm sure, millions of pages' worth of published and homemade mythology and backstory, game mechanics, sexy weapons, expanding and being added to all the while. It is a breathing system, growing as more play it and add to its lore. The attraction of the geas spell is one of control, one of the attractions of role-playing games at all, of attaining power over others, of commanding them.

The hellhound quotes are from those *Dragon* magazines, a monthly periodical devoted to role-playing games, particularly *D&D*. My parents' basement contained, until I rescued them, issues 75–130 of the magazine. Many pages are dog-eared or show drool or other obvious signs of my devotion. My favorite sections in the magazine are the ones where serious players write in and passionately query or debate obscurities, such as the hellhound discussion.

———

So as I am editing the essay on Gygax's death, Dave Arneson, Gygax's *D&D* somewhat-lesser-known cocreator, also dies. According to a statement from Wizards of the Coast, new owners of *D&D,* Arneson "developed many of the fundamental ideas of role-playing: that each player controls just one hero, that heroes gain power through adventures, and that personality is as important as combat prowess." This maps to the idea of memoir, in which the writers (or writers as characters) are typically cast as the heroes of their own lives, their own stories. They battle medical conditions, social mores, shifting cultural landscapes, their terrible fathers, whatever, and in the end they triumph.

The rise of the memoir correlates with the rise of role-playing games in the public consciousness,[†] the rise of fantasy role-playing in sexual situations, or in dramatherapy or psychotherapy. We are increasingly a culture raised on games. Sure, the idea of the hero isn't recent, nor are the story arcs that readers continue to desire. But the idea of role-playing as a formative game experience, of playing the role of a character in a fictional world, does make us more likely to consider our own roles in our own lives, to think of our lives in game terms.

In a sense Arneson's idea that personality is more important than "combat prowess" also correlates with memoir. When we write our memoirs we create characters of ourselves. We have to. And all this coincides with the further rise of the culture of the individual, with a generation growing up playing first-person shooters, actually visually experiencing another person's point of view, or trying out personas on social networking sites. And yes, we've always done these things (essays are virtual realities, as are books, and grade and high schools are sites of social networking, of role-playing, where we are expected to try out our various selves for public consumption). Still, if we think of our lives as oppositional, in story terms, with protagonists and antagonists, those archenemies who tormented us, those lovers who broke us, then it's easier to think memoir, to think of our lives as increasingly approaching a massively multiplayer role-playing game.

Or maybe we have grown so used to these immersive fictions that we have elevated the memoir to its new status in search of something more evidently true. And clearly we *enjoy* the game of spotting the bogus memoirs, of finding the hoaxes. It's hard not to see the Frey dustup as game, or the spate of more recent outings of increasingly hilarious fake memoirs as big-game hunting. And the fakers, the fudgers, we cast them as villains, antagonists. They are not lawful good. We are. We are righteous. Our job as readers is to root them out and triumph over them.

Am I really the only one who is enjoying this?

Unsurprisingly, Wizards of the Coast frames Arneson's death as game in their official obituary: "Dave Arneson, co-creator of the original *Dungeons & Dragons* game, passed away on Tuesday evening, April 7th, after waging one final battle against cancer." Another website,[†] Ars Technica, runs a story titled "Between Battles, the Story: Dave Arneson Has Passed On." The *Sci-Fi Wire* says: "after a long battle with cancer," etc. Another story follows up, framing his death as a game event: "Arneson lost a long battle with cancer last night."

Blizzard, the company responsible for the online RPG World of Warcraft, dedicated *WoW* patch 3.1.0 (an update to the game software) to Arneson. After the dedication, the patch notes swiftly descend (as patch notes will do, and as RPG-type people will do) into a kind of hilarious esoterica. These quotes are selected at random:

"Applying a glyph no longer requires a Lexicon of Power."

"Due to significant talent tree revisions, all players will have their talent points reimbursed."

"Command (Orc Racial): Applies to shaman pets, and now correctly applies to death knight pets."

"The shaman's Fire Elemental and Spirit Wolves, mage's Water Elemental and Mirror Images, and druid's Treants have all gained avoidance from area-of-effect damage similar to what warlock and hunter pets already have."

"Many Northrend maces now make correct noises when sheathed and unsheathed."

"Shadowmeld: Using this ability will no longer cause friendly players to deselect the night elf."

Thanks, Dave Arneson, Gary Gygax, for allowing us to make a life of this.

Version 4.0 of the *Advanced Dungeons & Dragons* rules comes out in six days on July 8, 2008. The version I played mostly was 2.0 (the version after *D&D*—the simpler version—was split into two, the simpler *D&D* and a more complex *advanced AD&D*; in general, among nonexperts, *D&D* refers to any of these versions), and I haven't paid any attention to the state of all things *D&D* since I stopped playing shortly before I went to college. I did not have a falling-out with the game, but it just became less fun to me, like it occured to me that there were, at last, at least, other things to do. I played one role-playing game (or tried to; we got bored and then drunk and then it was over) in grad school, and I tried out a session of *Vampire,* which came out when I was in college, with two guys who demanded that you call them in real life (not in game) "Pasha" and "Ghost," their given names too banal to bother with. They played with some goth girls (*Vampire* attracted the goth girls like nothing else), which was sexy in theory, but there were no capes or bodices, there was probably too much Concrete Blonde being used as sound track, and the experience was, on the whole, a bore.

I don't know if I was ever a very good player of *D&D* or any role-playing game. I was always the Dungeon Master, responsible for the creation of the fictional world and for refereeing the play of the game. The storytelling aspect must have appealed to me (and still does), but I've only played a character a handful of times, and I was not good at playing the role, which is a huge part of what makes RPGs fun, or so I am told. My brother and I both played, and we attended the yearly Gen-Con convention (the big convention for RPGs in America), which took place in Milwaukee, Wisconsin, close to the birthplace of TSR. My brother and I played at the convention, but I remember being too young, among a bunch of college kids and older people, and not really getting it. My father surely deserves an award for indulging our nerdery and taking us to the convention, but the game I saw wasn't the same as the game we played. These people were serious, I remember thinking; they were adults. Mostly I remember the fries at one of the Milwaukee malls as I stuffed them into my mouth. They were thick cut, natural, with bits of potato skin, covered in salt. And they came from a real Milwaukee mall, not a chickenshit little mall like our hometown Copper Country Mall, where the biggest store for four hours was a JC Penney.

Maybe it's more about control. The Dungeon Master makes the rules, knows all, or as much as is possible to know. It was hard for me to be just a player, with a more limited knowledge base, trying to inhabit a character. Maybe it was teenage solipsism, an inability or reluctance to inhabit anyone else. But reading gives the lie to this—that is the function of books, to allow us to inhabit another mind.

You can go to the website of Wizards of the Coast to learn all about *D&D.* Watching their online demo for how *D&D* is played is a very weird experience for this former player. For one, a girl is involved. That happened rarely. A couple of girls played with us a couple of times, including one who was later murdered (sad to think of her only in these terms—as murdered girl), but for the most part we were male, juvenile (we were juveniles who were especially juvenile). Various rape fantasies were probably deployed. My memory tastefully omits this. There was looting. Battles. You know. That's what you get with a duplex kitchen full of twelve-year-olds eating powdered sugar out of the bag, possibly because it looked a little bit like cocaine.

Version 4.0 incorporates a board-game element (the dungeons through which the players canter and saunter and creep are 2-D, visual, and the players are represented by pieces, miniature elves and wizards). The rules have been revamped to be significantly less technical. This sucks: a big part of the pleasure was in its headiness, its esoterica. Even looking at it, moving the dorky miniature representations of characters, feels reductive; it diminishes the imaginative qualities of the game. Are we getting more stupid? Does this make it an easier sell to parents, less transgressive with media fantasies of deranged kids running through steam tunnels under Michigan State University, taking drugs and fucking, and fighting each other with homemade foils fashioned from cut-off golf clubs? Or maybe "game" has become increasingly visual, requiring more consumption, more procuring and painting of miniatures, as if to better compete with the immersive quality of video role-playing games, or even memoirs?

*

"Controversy over the athcoid [more commonly known as the gelatinous cube] has long raged among the wise—quite heatedly so in the corridors of the Hall of Beast-Tamers and in the offices of the Imperial Zoo of Amn, the keepers of which have managed to keep a cube alive in captivity for some 12 winters. Over and over, the questions are asked: How intelligent are the cubes? How amorphous are their forms? Of what is their digestive fluid composed, and can it be used as a weapon or in alchemy (or, for that matter, in medicine or in the handling of beasts)? How do athcoids mate—indeed, *do* athcoids mate?" ("The Ecology of the Gelatinous Cube: Unseeing, Unthinking, Unstoppable," by Ed Greenwood, *Dragon* #124)

*

Many of my friends have mated. I have mated. I recommend it. *D&D* types mate consistently, often with other gamers. They have Renaissance Faire weddings, *World of Warcraft* weddings, Call of Cthulhu weddings. My wife dressed up as a wench for a friend's wedding in college. Said friend's Olde Marriage lasted less than a year.

Chivalry Sports is what appears to be a sporting goods store in central Tucson. It specializes in reproduction or semiperiod regalia for Renaissance Faires, and live action role-playing (LARP), and probably everything in between or on the spectrum of this culture, including meeting up with the "girl" you've been chatting with on *World of Warcraft* or on one of the more hardcore, old school, geek chic MUDs (multi-user dungeons), all text, a precursor of *Everquest* and *WoW* and other MMPORGs (massively multiplayer online role-playing games), which you likely know because you wonder about your friend, the addict to this game, this representation of reality, this particular version of life.

I pick up a poorly printed flier for the "Empire of Chivalry and Steel," a live-action medieval recreation society[†] that holds a number of medieval tournaments in which you can fight, craft, sing, and so on. From the website: "The Kingdom of Galandor is the first recognized Sovereign Territory of The Empire of Chivalry and Steel (ECS), Inc., founded on April 10, 1990. Our Kingdom encompasses all of Arizona, with an outlying territory in Illinois. We currently have three territories in our Kingdom: the Marquisate of Altiora (Tucson, AZ), the Marquisate of Solaris (Phoenix, AZ), and the Province of Northwatch (Chicago, IL)." You can find out more about them at Galandor.org.

Don't get me wrong—this is by no means *Dungeons & Dragons*. We didn't dress up . . . much . . . and if we did, and we held battles in friends' backyards with homemade wooden swords, then that wasn't *D&D* either but a natural, perfectly healthy, aerobic, enjoyable, undorky, unembarrassing offshoot of our interests. At Chivalry Sports you can certainly buy swords ("Practical Katana and Wazikashi," Scramasax, Main Gauche and Cup Hilt Rapier, Viking Swords, etc.), but it's mostly about the period outfits. You can buy a variety of T-shirts sporting logos of dragons ("Night Dragon," "Golden Dragon," "Breakthrough Dragon," "Black Dragon," "Dragon Whisperer," "Draco Basilica," "Whitby Worm," and "Wyverex Cipher" among others), pirate skulls, fairies ("Forest Meadow Fairy," "Purple Fairy") along with corsets, breeches for little boys, a "Children's

Commoner's Vest," a "Knightly Fighting Surcoat," "Druid Robe," and more. The catalog models tend to be a little fuller-figured, and the dudes have longer hair. There are a lot of apparently period-appropriate goatees. You can outfit your teddy bears with a variety of "Mini-Helms," and of course the books on medieval weddings are legion.

This collective devotion to re-creating the esoterica of this former culture is admirable. Glorious, even. I don't pretend that this is entirely due to *Dungeons & Dragons,* or due to Gygax, since after all fantasy literature has been around since time immemorial, and even the Society for Creative Anachronism (you know, those kids you see dressed up and battling in armor on college campuses) has been around since 1966, where it originated reportedly (the provenance of this quote is questionable) as "a protest against the twentieth century." Perhaps all these spawned gameworlds are a reaction against the undramatic life of so many (look who's talking, writer, reader, bore) today. The documentary film *Darkon* focuses on the related Darkon Wargaming Club, and specifically the lives of those engaged in a form of live-action *D&D,* the aforementioned LARP, contrasting the "regular" office, married, Walmart lives of the players with those of their rather more spectacular characters. It's beautiful and hilarious and also more than a little moving to watch them go at it, in the way that watching anyone completely lost in a world—whether fantasy, online, computer gaming, sporting, or whatever—can be. You have to admire the complex and complete lack of self-consciousness, the commitment to the rules and procedures and limits of the world. It's as if they exceed, transcend themselves each minute they play as someone else, as if they become deities, so far beyond the rest of self-conscious us that they barely matter to us, or us to them.

*

Backing out of Chivalry Sports onto the road, I realize there is a three-inch grasshopper in the center of my windshield. It's obscene, so splayed, so *there,* such a *fact.* I have a great view of its petticoat if not its genitalia as I accelerate to traffic speed. It seems almost happy as I push out of the city proper and toward the foothills, my speed increasing toward 60 mph. It remains, a gargoyle, a bastion, a bulkhead, uncaring. Usually insects on the windshield are sheared off pretty quickly, but this one is stalwart. It has an extremely high constitution, or maybe it just hits its saving throws. When I hit 64 mph, the grasshopper slowly starts to rotate so it faces forward, like a figurehead, Leonardo DiCaprio in *Titanic*, a dog with its face in the wind, wild, eating air. I have no capacity for comprehending the grasshopper brain, or what passes for a brain in a grasshopper (ganglia, loose groups of nerve cells, appear in each section of the grasshopper, though there is a brainlike cluster in the head), but it is still somehow awesome to watch. It is exceeding its natural capacity for speed (they can fly 8 mph) by eight times via the context of my car. At any moment I expect it to be blown off, confused, forced to go aloft, and to return to whatever grasshoppers do for fun or sustenance, if there is a difference. I drive four miles North[†] to the coffee shop where I am planning on working on this essay, and once I pull into the parking spot gently, so as not to dislodge it, having carried it so far with me, it straightens, turns with what appears to be dignity. It slowly climbs to the top of my car, beyond my vision, beyond anyone's vision or capacity for understanding, and disappears.

VANISHING POINT: CITY[†]

Cities of our past are like layers of paint underneath this one, waiting to be exhumed from memory:[†] the new city is conceived in terms of the old. Terra Cotta, the new restaurant we eat at in Tucson, is the new Bistro Bella Vita. The Blue Willow breakfast joint, the new Cherie Inn. We stamp the past on the present, a series of equivalencies, a set of mathematical transformations from one landscape to the next. The good thing about the new city is that it is geographically dissimilar to any place[†] we have lived in before. Moving from Madison, Wisconsin, to Iowa City, Iowa, for instance, is not so different: university towns with their hipsters and hippies and cultural capital, small midwestern state to small midwestern state. Rural to rural. Sun-spattered trees thick with humidity and the smell of huge farms. But Michigan to Arizona is an opposition, the erasure of one with the other. The sky is different, the weather patterns alien. Weather in the Southwest appears to move North[†] up from Mexico, far from the easy northeast motion through Chicago to Grand Rapids.

*

5751 N. Kolb Rd, #20204, Tucson, AZ 85750

Before 6 am and the world is bright and warmed already. On the balcony of our condominium (that glorious, temporary, vacationing word) in Tucson we stare at a manufactured landscape that apes the natural. The complex's edge consists of a rock wall that appears to have been cut or blown out of whatever was here before, but is, according to the civil engineer we have consulted, poured concrete in this natural-looking mold, complete with the unfinished look and the hexagonal patterns of cracks that act as a retaining wall. If Michigan, the Midwest, is flat grids of roads punctuated by the city, then Arizona is a series of subdivisions and manufactured walls set among mountain ranges.

The experience is one of immense space.[†] The downtown's smaller than the other former city, though the city is twice the size. Why bother with erecting high-rises or skyscrapers when you are cradled in four mountain ranges? In the other former city the buildings suggest a shelter from the openness. In this one architecture is of the landscape. In this one the architecture defeats the landscape. People roll out lawns to re-create their former cities, and thus their former lives, plant huge deciduous trees, splice together fruit salad trees out of lemon, lime, and kumquat trees so that they deliver a series of different fruits on different branches. This city is a place of reinvention. This city is designed away from the Eisenhower system of interstates.

A young faculty member we meet is from Bangalore, India. He bemoans the lack of public transportation, the heat.

In the foothills leading up to the Catalina Mountains the rich have made their homes. Their compounds are beautiful and elaborate. We don't know these lives. We don't know the lives of those living in the barrio down by the old downtown either.

In the city we are a we, collective, pressed together. We don't want to agitate for it, this particular living, since the country treats us well too, but here we can glissando by these other lives, impenetrable, unpredictable, and no one asks us what we are doing. We could be anything—terrorists, homeless, breathless.

*

From the eighth floor of the Meinel Optical Sciences building at the University of Arizona we overlook the North half of the campus, all brick and steel and white painted or whitewashed (is there a difference?) roof. This space, unlike the Midwest, is bounded. The Tucson mountains rise to the west. The Catalinas tower directly ahead over the foothills. We can't see the other two ranges (the Santa Ritas, the Rincons) from this vantage point, but the experience of space is one of boundaries. The sky, true, is limitless, we imagine, but it doesn't appear to stretch beyond the mountains, or if it does, which we know it does, we can't see it, so it might as well not exist, and this being a campus just before the semester's started, the view is one of possibility. Students are starting to be orientated, to learn their physical orientation, and you can see them being led around. They ask us where room 512 is and we tell them. They will continue to ask for the next whatever. We don't know where room 512 is but we bet it's on the fifth floor, we say, hoping we sound knowledgeable, or, failing that, helpful. This is our orientation. We are above them, it, the matrix of them that rapidly becomes an it. Trick of the space and perspective. The city here is laid out on a grid, and so from above the streets—Cherry and Third—run North and east until they disappear, and their traces are only suggested by the gaps in trees and buildings.

The campus itself is or at least approaches theory. Big research is being done here, we're told. The rhetoric of the buildings—steel and glass and some buried underground—tells us.

We like spaces best when we don't know our way around in them. There is a learning curve. *You are in a darkened room. You can barely see the edges. A door leads west. A door leads east. There is a chandelier.* This is all we know. We could be in a video game, or a situation allegedly connected to video games, with a campus shooter, nostalgically up in a clock tower. Or crawling through a dungeon[†] somewhere in the future. We are beginning to know this space but there's so much to know. What's in, for instance, the Bear Down Gymnasium that is no longer being used? The Corleone Apartments? El Portal? The Esquire? The Gitting Expansion? Herring Hall? The House Energy Doctor? The Institute for the Study of Planet Earth? The ever-present on college campuses of a certain age Old Main? These are unlit corners of the map. This space is all potential, question, a subject of a quest.

The same goes for the city, which holds its thousand thousand secrets and will not let them loose, not yet. And the mountain ranges catapulting up around it, and the space beyond that with its cavalcades of mines and military planes?

One city is inside the other city. South Tucson is one square mile in area, completely enclosed by Tucson. There is a story inside this story. There is a city inside the story inside the city. We are in the story, you and I, together, exploring.

The contents of one handmade box on my shelf: one Precious Moments figurine, received as a kind of semi-ironic wedding present. One packet, opened, of desiccated Listerine PocketPaks Freshburst breath strips that remind me of the strips of Doublemint my grandmother would always enclose in cards or letters to my brother and me, that would always arrive hard and broken. Thirty large paper clips. Six variously sized binder clips. A bunch of fantasy figurines: the skeleton king, several trolls, a laughing, axe-wielding dwarf. A broken microcassette sent to me anonymously, postmarked Nebraska City,[†] Nebraska: a mystery. An engraved Leatherman multitool from my grandmother. A "Wooden Nickel" from the Wooden Nickel Saloon in Marshall, Minnesota, good for one happy hour special drink. One flattened bag of "Toasted Corn" Doritos. One center-punch used for breaking windows on Michigan Bell trucks in Southfield, Michigan, and possibly for countersinking nails in my new bathroom wall. Most of the head of a plaster leopard, broken. One railroad spike from a no-longer operational line in my hometown. Actual evidence of an actual life. What meaning do these objects have? I have kept them for years now. What self do they conjure up? What stories do they tell?

TRAN-SUB-STANTI-ATION

> *Doritos The Quest:*
> *$100,000 in treasure awaits the victor*
> *Many Will Try*
> *Only One Will Succeed*
> *Guessing the flavor is just the beginning.*
> —the DoritosTheQuest.com website[†]

"On 12th June 2008, your ad will be broadcast across the universe from the Svalbard 500 MHz Ultra High Frequency Radar station. This Norwegian space[†] research base is situated on Svalbard Island between Norway and the North[†] Pole. Your ad will be broadcast for 24 hours to a range of solar systems, some of which have planets that theoretically could support life" (from the Doritos "You make it, we play it" website).

I love the audacity of Doritos, or the company that has made them for nearly fifty years, Frito-Lay. Aside from the incontrovertible fact that boxes of bags of Doritos are much lighter to transport than Fritos, which have a much greater density (I know this from

I learned to hate Fritos for this reason that summer, though working in a Frito-Lay warehouse for a summer unloading semis filled with snacks), Doritos have a delicious and hilarious majesty. Even if I don't love them, I admire them. They are the perfect modern snack, honed by forty-two years of snack-making technology (they debuted in America in 1966 along with the Society[†] for Creative Anachronism: clearly 1966 was a banner year for strange Americana), ideally salty, artificially[†] flavored, and addictive as anything I can conceive of that is permitted by law, and possibly more addictive than a number of narcotics. (In fact, the two often go together.) Frito-Lay is a player; it dominates the chip market, being responsible for most of the chips you likely ingest or think about ingesting, ogling in the towering megasupermarket aisles on your angry weekly trip with your passel of kids in tow, or, alone, watching those characters bicker with their partners and kids and harvest tins of whatever into their biggie-sized carts.

I have a thing for things that taste[†] like other things. The ambiguity this sentence suggests is, I hope, pleasing. The most recent love of mine in this category is the Doritos X-13D "experimental flavor" chips from 2007 that identified themselves as a mystery "All-American Classic" flavor, which tasted quite close to actual charbroiled Burger King burgers. I appreciate the modern magicianship here: you put a chip (itself a form of modern processing magic) in your mouth and it tastes like a cheeseburger, grill flavoring, pickles, yellow mustard, ketchup, onions, and all. I am drawn to the Listerine (and other) pocket pack strips that transform to flavor inside your mouth. It is transubstantiation, the transformation from one substance to another, or at least its effect. I'm not Catholic so for me growing up Communion was always symbolic, perplexing, and awkward. Grape juice and flavorless wafers periodi-

my often-baked friends learned to love me for my ability to bring them unlimited supplies of Fritos, mostly. We would throw out boxes and boxes of the snack-sized bags each day that were within two days[†] of their expiration date, which really means almost nothing in this processed, fortified, and preservatived world. So I brought them home all the time. This did not help my weight. My friend Leonard and I threw hundreds of surplus bags of them out of our twelfth-story apartment window one night just before we moved out. I am not proud of this. Or maybe I am since I am relating it. It was beautiful watching them flutter to the earth below or lodge themselves in trees, a confetti layer of glittering packaging covering the earth. Like that Sherwin-Williams campaign with the tagline "Cover the Earth" featuring an image of a bucket of Sherwin-Williams paint dousing the globe with a color that looks like blood.

cally placed on my adolescent tongue were strange in that I entered into this other (adult, mysterious) world of meaning and connotation, but it wasn't reverent. It wasn't exciting, fun. Of course I had never really been particularly religious, so it was simply a ritual for me, strange and empty as anything.

The fact that Doritos is beaming a commercial into space, into a system forty-two light-years away, makes me unusually happy. It is retarded, of course, but also grand in the obtuseness of its conceit, and it spawned the following quotation from the UK *Telegraph* news website: "'In this case we are giving somebody the opportunity to create this message as a way to say hello on behalf of mankind,' says Prof van Eyken, who adds the prospect of the Earth being destroyed by Doritos hating aliens is remote. 'No, I am not worried.'" It would, of course, be ironic if this was the first contact made between us and another planet, but it is, as are most events in terms of astronomy, including potential annihilation, highly remote.

The winning commercial is called "Tribe" and features stop-motion animation of individual Doritos chanting in a circle and worshipping a jar of Doritos salsa in its center.

I don't know if Frito-Lay makes the best snacks, really, because they're so ubiquitous. I have never been given the option of deciding if Doritos are any good at all in my life. They have always just been there lining both sides of the grocery store snack aisle, and if I wanted chips, chances are good that they were made by Frito-Lay. I had thought Lays and Ruffles and Doritos and Fritos were in competition with each other, had some kind of East Coast–West Coast hip-hop rivalry going, only to find they were all made by the same company, and that any sense of competition was entirely created, a marketing maneuver, a strategy.

Their newest promotion is the aforementioned Doritos: The Quest, which again presents a mystery flavor to American audiences, and apparently we find this irresistible. I do, certainly. There is pleasure in trying new products for me, overconsumer as I am, so I will almost always try a new flavor of a product I am familiar with: M&Ms, for instance (the crispy M&Ms in the light blue bag—not to be confused with the dark chocolate in the dark blue bag—are great). Any new flavor, no matter how unappealing-seeming. Those Jones sodas flavored for Thanksgiving: turkey, cranberry, green bean, stuffing—even these don't seem excessive. Or, well, sure they're excessive, but that makes them irresistible. It is the natural end point of artificial flavors. If they weren't so expensive I would have bought them when they came out. It's the geek in me, the early adopter of new technologies, or the explorer, the one who sometimes wants so badly to be first to try the beer of everyone at the table that I'll take a surreptitious sip while toting them back from the bar. This probably doesn't speak well of me and my evident desire for assumed authority.

My admiration for transubstantiation comes from my desire to occasionally obliterate myself and become something/someone else. To metamorphose. To transform. To alchemically recompose, to look like a thing and taste like or sound like something else. Fifty percent of the times I answer the phone to a telemarketer, I am addressed as "Miss" or "Mrs." I don't know why.

Since the trashy Circle K up the street carries Doritos The Quest chips in addition to their full wall of 40s of malt liquor flavored like lemonade or passionfruit or energy drinks or beer, I buy two bags and consume one on the walk home. The bags are black, with an electrical-looking design that probably passes for *mysterious*. Like most Doritos, they explode in your mouth: your saliva activates the MSG immediately and you might as well not try to eat anything else besides the rest of the bag for a couple of hours. In fact, you'll try to keep recovering the flavor of those first couple of bites for the rest of the bag, with your taste buds gradually losing their sensitivity.

The first note is an obvious lime, like the Tostitos Hint of Lime chips I like. That's too simple, though. I give one to my wife. She and I agree: margarita, right? That's closer, but still not quite right. I doubt Doritos would have an alcoholic-drink-flavored chip, and besides the finish is too sweet to be margarita. I go on the website to try *Margarita*, which is not correct. However, I try a couple of other things, ending with *Mountain Dew* as the correct flavor. The chips do, I think, taste something like Mountain Dew (like Frito-Lay, owned by Pepsico). We purchase a one-liter of Mountain Dew to taste-test, and yes, and then that rush. I hadn't had Mountain Dew or dew from any mountain (what a great linguistic package that name is! The Faygo brand had a knockoff flavor of it called Moon Shine, which they later changed to Moon Mist; of course Mello Yello doesn't get close to the obnoxiousness of Mountain Dew, the original, not the Code Red or its new variation as an energy drink, or any of the rest of the diaspora—it's amazing, isn't it, watching the brand growth, the flavor variations, triple, quintuple, grow exponentially, as the marketing department wants something *new* to sell?) in maybe ten years. I will admit it is delicious. I also wouldn't have identified Mountain Dew as lime-flavored, but clearly, on tasting, that's one of the initial components. The drink tastes like the chips. The drink does not make me want more of the chips. Or of the drink.

I don't care enough, though, to embark upon THE QUEST. I imagine I have to give them my address, which I'd rather not, creeped out by the spread of our personal information everywhere and the spam calls I keep getting on my cell phone, and they'll send me some free coupons for crap I don't really want. As exciting as this is, and as much as I would like $100,000, I'm too disillusioned by consumer society to expect to have any chance at winning. Plus the website's Flash component doesn't really work right on my computer, and I get annoyed, as pretty as the artwork is. It is enough to taste the Mountain Dew–flavored chips, to have identified them, and to move on to something new.

As far as odd chip flavors go, though, a visit to an Asian grocery garners you some encounters with really whacked-out chips. After all, sushi—an amazing collision of flavor: fish, seaweed, rice, ginger, soy, wasabi!—comes from the East. China carries both "Nacho Cheese" and "Rock Taco" flavors of Doritos. Canada, melting pot that it is, has "Red Hot Reiner" (?) and "Tandoori Sizzler." Australia carries a "Tapas" flavored chip, flavored, I presume, like expensive appetizers served in tiny portions to fancy people. The Netherlands carries "Cool American" (Cool Ranch), "Honey Roasted," and "Pure Paprika" flavors. The slogan on their website is "Doritos. Yiiiiiha!" The diaspora of Doritos flavors is the spread of our culture across the globe. It is regrettable and great in equal proportion, this separating of actual taste from actual food resulting in transubstantiative magic. In this way beaming a Doritos commercial into outer space is quite possibly an excellent representative of our culture.

I am pickier about food than I want to be, and it takes me a long time to come around to new foods. I am very often in the awkward social position of explaining to friends and dinner companions why I don't like duck, for example, or won't eat lamb, or mushrooms, or walnuts. It's less a sense of *not liking* than it is about *won't eat* for most of them. I am not interested in eating any meats beyond my current contingent of them (beef, pork, turkey, chicken, fish—any fish, really, I'm open to, though I'm less interested in octopus, squid, oysters, crap with shells or tentacles, a multiplicity of eyes, tendrils, etc.). It is probably a desire to disassociate the food from the animal. I will try new vegetables, though I will not like them. It's the substance, the emotional memory[†] of a food. The texture usually rather than the taste. I imagine mushrooms to taste okay to maybe good, but the texture doesn't work for me.

But in terms of *flavor*, I will try anything. Once you disassociate the flavor from the food, the flavor floats up, the word lonely and getting stranger in the sentence without the sensation or connotation of actual *food*. The food is my objection. If I had lived in the sixties, I would be in good shape with their vision of how we would eat in the future. In 1962 the French weekly *l'Express* predicted, "By the year 2000 all food will be completely synthetic. Agriculture and fisheries will have become superfluous," according to Paleo-future, a blog devoted to this subject. Food via cube or dissolving strip or vitamin pill or any of the things that potentially make the act of eating an act simply of nutrient and flavor consumption. In some ways we have achieved this future. Don't think the chemical magic of Cool Whip as much as high-fructose corn syrup and Yellow 5 Lake, chloroisothiazolinone, and the dozens of unrecognizable chemical strings in most branded, packaged food you can buy in stores. We have steadily moved away from the idea of pill as food, but we've fortified our breads, put the pill into the food, packed our orange juice with Omega-3, made the food look more foodlike, slapped "natural" and "heart-healthy" on everything, though it's filled with nonfood ingredients. The organic, local, slow food movement responds to this, but its presence as a reaction suggests the dominant culture, that the key innovation of food technology over the last decade is to recognize that consumers still want the experience of eating food that looks like food but we don't really care how much it actually is like food. Food's hard. Kind of gross. Difficult to transport and grow without pesticides. So make it *like* food. It should smell and taste like food, but more so: it's food but jacked way up with MSG and salt and sugar and chemical goodness.

Doritos are clearly not a food at all but a food system. A system that contains food, but also incorporates health claims, marketing, artificial flavor, manufacturing—food not as product but as process, continually in motion. The Doritos The Quest flavor succeeds by making the consumer an explorer, an Indiana Jones of crappy, awesome snacks. Eating becomes a game, a first-person shooter, each bite an artificial landscape, overlaid by a website where you get clues and search for the treasure. It is speculative, exciting. A challenge. I could get into this. Of course if you'd never had Mountain Dew, if you weren't a good consumer, how could you possibly succeed?

Doritos have a "Toasted Corn" flavor that is unfortunately unavailable in Michigan. It is, however, available in my new home of Tucson, Arizona, a city[†] packed with tortilla options. I buy a bag in Basha's, the upscale grocery store in the foothills of the Catalina Mountains filled with well-off, tan people in shorts and skirts shopping with small carts. It's fun to watch the Doritos marketing department try to find a way to snazzify and make extreme the simple fried corn tortillas seasoned with salt, what all their chips are, at base. The bag reads: "Rip open a bag of the Doritos brand toasted corn tortilla chips you crave. Experience that powerful Doritos brand crunch together with the tasty flavor of toasted corn in your mouth. It's the only snack bold enough to call itself Doritos." Except it's all in caps in what looks like a proprietary Exciting Doritos font. *Powerful* and *Bold* are in red. The list of ingredients on this seemingly basic flavor of Doritos omits the litany of artificial-sounding polysyllabic chemicals. I'm a little bit surprised that the marketing copy hasn't pitched these chips as "Natural," which is the usual method with nonartificially flavored chips. At least 90 percent of the chips available in Basha's snacks aisle are Frito-Lay products. Snyder's pretzels are an exception, as are Poore Brothers chips (made by Inventure, based in Phoenix, Arizona), and a local brand of corn tortilla chips. The toasted corn chips are a pretty good mouth experience, but they are oddly lacking. You put the chip in your mouth and, what, no explosion of flavor? Au contraire, they have the texture and crunch of Doritos but they don't do what Doritos normally do. They just sort of sit there, untransfigured, untransformed.

*

I like to provide my friends with new flavors of Doritos. I like Doritos. I like to be the purveyor of new flavors. I might as well work for them, get a commission. A Dorito solo is a sad thing, but bagged, en masse, wrapped with language and imagery, they are delicious. They are abundance. Artificiality defined, since they are shaped like nothing natural: who invented the nearly equilateral triangle shape of these things? They are by design egalitarian; you can pick them up by any corner and stuff them by handfuls in your mouth. They don't taste like anything in nature. Possibly I am expecting my role to be this: provider of hilarious food products to skeptical friends. Cheerleader for unpopular snacks. I have a soft spot for unpopularity, the failed experiment. Sad product, the multiplication of texture and chemical flavor, I hold you to my chest. I collect you. I will catch you when you fall. Everyone else hates the X-13D Doritos I pushed on them last year, the vegetarians especially, when I realized they had beef tallow in them and was honor-bound to inform them of my (and Frito-Lay's) transgression. I don't love them obsessively, because I like my health enough to know better, but I do admire fallen things. Discontinued sodas (available via the soda collector's website sodafinder.com) like Sunkist Lemonade, highly valued by my wife, or Cheerwine, Moxie, Pepsi Clear, Coke 2, and so on. The simple act of cataloging these hard-to-find products is a form of heroism. Making them available for connoisseurs, even better.

*

The El Matador Tortilla Factory, a local tortilla chip manufacturer, sits just on Grand Rapids' southwest side, abutting a redesigned and fresh-looking housing project on the south, and a bunch of industrial-looking buildings on the North. The grounds are surrounded by barbed wire–trimmed fences angled inward, as if toward a prison. A FedEx semi drives into the parking lot as I sit awaiting the interview, and backs elegantly toward the shipping doors (which are not the same as the receiving doors on the other side of the building, implying that one is outgoing, I suppose, and the other in), stopping just short of them. It is a nice piece of driving. I am awaiting a meeting with Thomas Chriese at El Matador.

Inside, the El Matador retail store, a room off the tortilla factory, sells two or three varieties of their chips alongside a variety of Mexican food products, dried peppers, tostadas, hot sauces, beans. Peculiarly, they also have a cooler full of Clamato. The office of operations is nondescript. In the lobby there is a framed photo of the Navarros, who founded El Matador, hanging above a vase filled with artificial flowers. There's a small circular table with a plastic tablecloth, a map of Sandy Pines in Michigan, a photo of World War II–era soldiers storming an unnamed beach. A "We're So

Happy" smiley poster and a row of cups sit next to a tiny set of deer antlers mounted on a plaque shaped like a shield. There is a handful-sized bit of deer head attached to them and a bell dangling from the whole piece. Another matted photo's caption reads "Tortilla-maker, San Javier del Bac, Tucson, Arizona, 1988, #1." I sit at the table, adorned by Goya Salsita Piquant Smoky Ancho Chiles Hot Sauce, Goya Stick Cinnamon, a rolled-up bag of Garlic Bread Nibblers (made by Snyder, the pretzel makers), a plastic knife, and an empty plastic one-liter jar that appears to have been once filled with salt, judging from the encrusted remains.

The whole place[†] has the smell of tortilla chips, as you'd expect, fried, with salt, the sound of humming fans and a price gun being operated in the next room to price glossy bags of something. A Hispanic radio station plays in the background, which stays background since I can't understand the language.

Tom comes in with a beard-guard, a hair-guard, a 2003 Salsa something T-shirt, and jeans. I ask him to start with the history of El Matador, which he doesn't know much about since he just came here after they were purchased by Garden Fresh, located in Detroit. "The real story here is Garden Fresh," twelve years old and growing dramatically because of their focus on fresh, organic products, their salsa leading the way. They also make chips, hummus, and other things, and they purchased El Matador partly in order to use this facility's excess capacity to manufacture their own chips in response to overwhelming demand. What is the story? I wonder.

Tom tells me that Garden Fresh is doing so well because they're in an emerging market with "a breakthrough flavor profile." He hits this business-speak often during our conversation. He's most excited about marketing, how it's about people, "this

Flavor profile is one of several commonly used descriptive test methods for evaluating

human experience, multidimensional, psychology and sociology."

We talk in the side room, separated from the front office by a door with some Mayanlike carvings on it. This is obviously their multipurpose room. One corner is filled with boxes; foodstuffs are littered through it—a box of Quaker Oatmeal Squares, a table covered with tortillas from a local tortilleria, two canisters of Hint of Lime Tortilla Chip Seasoning by a company called Spicetec, a subsidiary of the creepily named but market-dominant ConAgra. Their online brochure boasts that "Spicetec's flavor technologists know that the essence of savory is multifaceted. It unites the five basic tastes . . . with volatile aromatics, Maillard reaction products, herbs, spices, and countless other elements to generate that sought-after 'just right' profile. Taking all of this into account, we design reliable, authentic and simply delicious taste systems for every application." The brochure goes on to state that their "propriety reaction-flavor technology captures and concentrates what makes beef taste like beef," and that "we custom-develop flavors across the full range of cooking techniques and degrees of doneness."

In spite of this extended immersion in artificiality, looking at the websites makes me hungry.

*

Inventure Group, Inc., based in Goodyear, Arizona, a suburb of Phoenix, makes three flavors of Burger King–branded snack chips. The "Flame Broiled Flavored Potato Snacks" feature "natural flavors, including grill" though apparently no beef tallow. They have the consistency of Tato Skins (the company also bought and continues to sell Tato Skins, those early '90s excellently named faux-potato-skin chips that

foods. Developed in the 1940s, it is still consistently one of the terms bandied about by food producers to describe their products. More from the Spicetec brochure: "We are experts in differentiated and nuanced savory profiles, creating a 'brothy' or 'roasted' chicken, or beef flavor from 'pot roast' to 'prime rib.' Our proprietary reaction-flavor technology captures and concentrates what makes beef taste like beef, and chicken taste like chicken." Other methods of descriptive testing include Texture Profile, Quantitative Descriptive Analysis, Time-Intensity Descriptive Analysis, and The Spectrum Descriptive Analysis Method. All of these methods use—or *utilize*, as they would probably put it, preferring a more technological-sounding term—humans, replete with the usual sorts of human error, though these humans have been selected and trained for panels analyzing flavor, texture, odor, and so on. Some of the sample questions that show up on prescreening questionnaires in the standard text on the Spectrum method (*Sensory Evaluation Techniques,* by Morton Meilgaard, Gail Vance Civille, and B. Thomas Carr) include the following: "Name some things that are sticky. What specific appearance characteristics of a bath tissue influence your perception of the feel of it? Which is thicker, an oily or a greasy film? What do you feel in a fabric or paper product they claimed were made with actual potato skins, which is doubtful if uninvestigated) and are not as appetizing as the X-13D chips. For starters, they lack the variety of obvious flavors when you put them in your mouth. They taste savory, and aren't bad, but you can't cycle through the flavors in the flavor profile quite as easily. They also lack actual meat fat. And they are not Doritos, which is a familiar experience in the mouth. You eat a Dorito, you know what to expect. These, you don't, so they're a complete unknown. A zero. A blank page.

Another flavor/food system/product is their "Onion Ring Snacks," which resemble the dried French onions you find on green bean casseroles in the Midwest for Thanksgiving, or, failing that, resemble Funyuns, which I used to love (and remember puking up a couple of times in my early teens, my then desire for consumption even greater than it is now, fat kid that I was and at heart, still am). I imagine they, like Funyuns, are incredibly gross in the mouth.

The last flavor (for now—I can only imagine these expanding further if they do well, like any consumer product, or virus) is "Ketchup & Fries Flavored Potato Snacks," which tastes mostly of ketchup and potatoes, presumably patterned after the success of ketchup-flavored potato chips in Canada, among other places. But these other flavors are the second tier in the brand. The fact that Burger King actually gave their name to these is sort of stunning, even as the commercials featuring the disturbing plastic replica homoerotic king show a talent for irony, enjoying their own freaky artificiality. It doesn't make me want Burger King, or food of any sort. These lack the magic.

The copy on the website (and the bag) for the flame-broiled snacks reads, in part: "Of course we're

that makes it feel stiff? If a recipe calls for thyme and there is none available, what would you substitute? What are some other foods that taste like yogurt? Why is it that people often suggest adding coffee to gravy to enrich it? Describe some of the notable flavors in: mayonnaise, cola, sausage, Ritz crackers. Describe some of the particles one finds in foods. How often in a month do you eat a complete frozen meal? How many weeks vacation do you plan to take between June 1 and September 30? What are some words which would describe the smell of a hamper full of clothes? Describe some of the noticeable smells in a: bar soap, basement, McDonald's restaurant?" Reading these questions makes me feel entirely insecure about my ability to perceive and qualify (much less quantify) differences in texture, odor, flavor, or the length of my summer vacation. Though I would dearly love to take part in a flavor profiling panel, my guess is that I'd be weeded out immediately (for, among other things, drinking too much coffee, which dulls your ability to taste[†] for up to an hour). This is an aside, sure, but it's incredibly interesting when you start getting inside an idea like this. Of course all this means that an incredible amount of testing has been done before products are released to the market. Which explains the popularity of the Burger King tacos, the wretched Burger King Iced talking about America's favorite burger: the flame-broiled, made-to-order WHOPPER®. Accept no imitations. Because no matter which of the 221,184 different ways you choose to customize it, you can bet you're getting it your way. That's what makes a WHOPPER® a WHOPPER®. Anything less is a massive disappointment." Such as these chips, which are by definition not a Whopper, and/or less than a Whopper. They are in fact less good than a Whopper, which I have been known to consume. Whoppers are good, both the burgers and the malted milk balls.

The ketchup and fries chips taste a lot like ketchup and fries. I imagine these flavors are easier to re-create/represent since the fast-food experience of eating fries in ketchup is already fairly processed: the fries are mashed and reconstituted (typically, in most fast-food joints), shaped, and fried, and ketchup is mashed, reconstituted tomatoes. And the fast-food experience is a step toward really fast food: chips in bags—food products that taste like other food products that resemble (superficially) actual foods (potatoes and tomatoes). My fast food just got faster. Now I can crack open the bag and snarf them down whenever I like. It's not quite astronaut freeze-dried ice cream, but it's getting there. Or maybe it's so far past there, and so in the midst of our everyday experience that we just don't notice it.

The Inventure Group is also responsible for such advances in snack technology as: T.G.I. Friday's Cheese Pizza Chips, Cheese Quesadilla Chips, and Cheddar & Bacon Potato Skins, Mozzarella Snack Sticks, Hot Pepper Jack Cheese Fries; Bob's Texas Style Sweet Maui Onion Potato Chips; Poore Brothers Sweet Chili & Red Pepper Flavor Chips and BBQ Ranch Chips; the aforementioned Tato Skins, which come in "Cheddar & Bacon Potato Skins" flavor, "Sour Cream & Onion Potato Skins" flavor,

Mocha Coffee Drink (not to ceaselessly pillory Burger King, which is certainly not the worst offender, even by fast food standards), and, among other things, the Doritos X-13D Tortilla Chips, no matter how much I personally enjoyed that experience.

Increasingly I have been questioning the usefulness or accuracy of my observations about my likes and dislikes, which would appear entirely arbitrary. I have recently come around to zucchini and olives (thanks to a former girlfriend) and I am even beginning to tolerate mushrooms (no thanks to my friend Nicole, who terrorizes me with them at any opportunity). One of the projects I've been working on is my thirty-third Birthday Mix† CD project, in which I asked a bunch of friends and acquaintances (and a few strangers) to make me a birthday mix CD (in lieu of a mixtape, which is purer but which I can no longer listen to since the great exodus of all my tapes a decade ago). I received over fifty and have been plowing through them, listening to and annotating each track. For someone who considers himself to be a serious enthusiast and geek of all things music, what I have been finding is that my apparent dislike of individual musicians or tracks is difficult to sustain when listening seriously to a track on my headphones, especially when it has been selected and "Original Potato Snack Chips" flavor (which the website describes, self-consciously, grandiosely, awesomely, as "an oasis of potato chip paradise"); the obviously upscale Boulder Canyon Tomato & Basil snack chips, the Boulder Canyon Rice & Adzuki Bean Natural Salt Artisan Snack Chips (which probably only comes in a tiny, gourmet bag), Balsamic Vinegar & Rosemary Potato Chips, Spinach and Artichoke Kettle Chips, Malt Vinegar and Sea Salt Chips, and so on. Clearly each new invented flavor adventure moves toward a new section of the grocery aisle, colonizing a new taste.

I'm sitting in my office chair crunching on the BK Flame Broiled chips, which aren't good, but, stocked with MSG as they are, they're addictive. I have nearly finished the bag, 450 calories (but zero grams of trans fat!) of excellence. I left a message for Steve Sklar, the Senior VP of Marketing at Inventure twenty minutes ago, since we had scheduled a conversation about their artificial snack foods, but I'm increasingly unconvinced he will call me back. At least the bag is nearly gone. I didn't expect him to be a big fan of his own chips, though being in marketing, he probably has to claim to be. On the Inventure homepage, http://www.inventuregroup.net, I find a hilarious photo. The whole website is populated by photos of smiling people, enjoying outrageous flavors. The ad copy for the group indicates that "The uniqueness of our flavors are [sic] only matched by our employees' passion for developing new and exciting snack foods." The website claims that the employees are "outrageously fun people." Perhaps this explains the photograph of five people of various races dancing together.

specifically for me. So my long hatred of "Sweet Home Alabama," for instance, just to give one example, inspired by far too much exposure to it when living in Tuscaloosa and attending occasional Crimson Tide football games—even that distrust of the song evaporates when I actually listen to it in the context of other songs. It's bearable. Enjoyable even, in a way. What this means for this sense of self that I have so carefully cultivated through strident disapproval of acts like the y-rich Lynyrd Skynyrd and Stone Temple Pilots and the Arctic Monkeys and Joni Mitchell—where that takes me I am not quite sure. If I can't be defined by my hatreds and antipathies, then *who* can I really say I am? And, worse, can I really say *I am?*

Very very unfortunately—or maybe perfectly, as if the image is so ephemeral it is made to be disposed of quickly—I can only find a low-res version of this, so it's included in all its pixelly goodness here:

It has clearly been assembled via Photoshop, since the woman in the back appears to be levitating. They are evidently very fun people, though they are models. A hazy blue ring circles them as if they were a planet, presumably to connote motion. Everyone in the faux photograph looks handpicked from 1980s music videos. The marketing department has taken several pages from the Mountain Dew playbook circa 1998. As a result, the magic is void, the curtain see-through. The flavor transformation, its transubstantiation from artificial crappy-looking chip to actual food eating experience ruined. I feel more hollow than I did before.

Perhaps deep in the bowels of their stock photo department, Inventure could deliver a high-resolution version? The production and delivery of stock photography, particularly a weirdo, dated stock photograph, is its own strange world. I contacted Inventure to find out the source of this image and the story behind it, but so far I have not yet heard back. Their beautiful surface—like any other, whether model, car body, or glistening shell—is difficult to actually communicate with.

The more I start to think about transubstantiated foods, the more I think of, and the more desire I have to try them again, you know, for research: Bacos, Tofurkey, not to mention Carnation Instant Breakfasts, Tang, and shots at the bar: Snickers, German Chocolate Cake, the incredible muchness that technology giveth. Or the Chinese specialty of Mock Duck (or mock pork/turkey/beef/etc., which is apparently a real probability). This could take me anywhere.

Later I track down some vegetarian chicken at Guilin Healthy Chinese Food in Tucson and, no surprise, it's pretty good. I have no idea what it is, but it's as good as chicken when you douse it in sauce for moo shu. I'd avoid the veggie ham, however.

Because I have been a somewhat squeamish eater all my life, I like bypassing the actual interaction with the natural world. Like kids text-messaging each other while standing in each other's body heat at the Tilly & the Wall concert at the Congress Club, or like the twenty-one-and-older crowd that has to stand behind the weird netting in the bar area, separated from the kids in front, I want the world interpreted, processed, managed, reduced. And the world comes packaged this way increasingly. Opportunities for intervention, for intercession between it and me, expand. Catholics ask saints for intercession on their behalf. Since I'm not religious, I have Doritos. I have BK-flavored snacks. I have engineers working deep

into the night on my behalf. I have marketing, assembled photographs of people dancing.

Like eating actual fries and ketchup, I have a hard
time stopping eating the BK fries & ketchup chips
before downing the bag. My wife is cooking actual
food in the other room but my stomach wants to be
filled with little food systems, little Frito-like chips
dusted in ketchup powder (or something) and MSG.

And writing about these things
increases my desire for them
significantly so I have been
eating stacks of junk for the
duration of this essay—and
the experience of the essay is
continually re-created as my
taste buds anticipate the coming flavor, even when reading
menus or reading about it or
calling it up from the queue of
memory.

*

It is a monsoon afternoon in Arizona, meaning that
spots of thunderstorms are expected all over the
foothills, where I am located and live for the time
being. Beautiful teenagers walk into the Subway in
front of me. These things have both become ubiquitous in our culture. When the first Subway opened in
my remote hometown, it was a sensation. The parking lot outside it was where teenagers went to gather
on summer or other evenings. But now thanks to the
formerly fat Jared, also ubiquitous and part of our collective psyche, Subways are everywhere. They pitch
themselves as the healthy option of fast food. These
teenagers are lithe, emo-framed, with oversized sunglasses, as is the trend. They are ordering five-dollar
footlongs inside and filling up their cups with foun-
tain Mountain Dew. Perhaps they might cross over
to the chips, this is the thinking. Earlier today I was
at the Titan Missile Museum† outside Tucson, the
only remaining cold-war era Titan Missile silo in the
world, or so they say. I have become less trusting of
claims made by anyone. I have become adult enough
to doubt. But this claim seems credible, the people
who staff it all volunteer, older men mostly, a little
crabby, distrustful of modern anything, and our tour
guide actually served inside the missile silo in the
'70s, or so he tells us (this too could be a prop—the

world is filled with them, props: we are being marketed to constantly, focus-grouped and told what it is thought we want to hear). The Titan missile is the largest nuclear ICBM ever in the U.S. active arsenal, and this one, like the others surely, is in the middle of nowhere. A little town with its prefab strip mall has sprung up around it, thirty miles from anywhere else resembling civilization.

The other Titan sites were in Kansas, Oklahoma, and Arkansas, sites of much nothingness. These are artifacts of our national hysteria for all things nuclear. They provide a dangerous edge to the middle of nowhere. On I-10 in New Mexico just before you hit the Arizona border you see a sign that reads "Exit 29" and then blankness. No highway name, no town name. There appears to be nothing else at this exit. No crossroad that I remember, but some sort of structure appears there. On extreme closeup via Google Earth it turns out to be the Lordsburg, New Mexico, pumping station. It looks just like one of those nothing structures that could be concealing a nuclear missile silo, like grain elevators dotting North Dakota that my brother and I speculated might too conceal instruments of war. The cold war brought us this distrust, this maybe teenage-boyish interest in speculating on spaces. It energizes the blanknesses that exist everywhere in America.

Lordsburg was one site of a Japanese American internment camp opened in 1942, and one of their sentries shot and killed two of the prisoners under questionable circumstances later on that year. There's not much else in Lordsburg, though it was popular for black travelers, being one of the few places in the Southwest with hotels that would accept them. Around it is yet more beautiful emptiness.

The Titan missile station that's in Sahuarita, Arizona, now exists only as a museum, a reminder of our former (and maybe current—the tour guide is adamant that the cold war is not over) fears. From above you would imagine it was nothing but a pumping station. But underneath the sixty-plus security features that would make it a "hard" area according to the Air Force (i.e., able to withstand a nuclear attack), you find something else entirely, a mecca of 1970s weapon technology. In less than two minutes the silo doors can be opened and the missile fired, and this blankness transformed.

In the gift shop they have nuke T-shirts and rocket-themed toys. I pick up a package of a freeze-dried astronaut ice cream sandwich. I haven't had one of these for years. In the '80s all my friends wanted these things, and the kid who got to go to Space Camp and brought back a handful for us was regarded as a king. And now I don't even remember his name. It, too, is a piece of history, an example of culinary magic. It's shrink-wrapped in a foil bag, ready for easy and potentially delicious deployment. This is the apex of so-called space-age food technologies, *astronaut food*, ice cream in particular, though freeze-dried ice cream was reportedly only used once in space (*Apollo 7*, 1968) before the astronauts lobbied against it. It's available in pretty much any science museum gift shop, and you or your kid has probably tried it or asked for it. It's also not very good, I imagine: a novelty, really. A thing you try once and buy for others only if they ask for it. Unlike the X-13D chips, which are no longer available, but are mourned, at least by me.

Opening the bag creates a rattling. The ice cream sandwich looks desiccated, though it looks like most other ice cream sandwiches I have had. I break a piece off for my wife; we are both hungry and this is what's available. One of the older women at the museum asked me if I'd eaten them before. Yes, I say, I have, but it's been awhile. She tells me not to chew it, but to let it dissolve on my tongue. She says they're gritty otherwise, like a carton full of tooth-shattering nuts, be careful. Okay, I say, thanks. I think of that when I open the package. Breaking off a piece, flakes of it catch air and I can see them floating down toward the carpet. I don't know what I expect here but it had better be good. This is childhood, a return to memory, but even so I don't remember what it tasted like then either. And children's taste buds aren't fully developed (hence the attraction to candy, Mountain Dew, to chips, sugar bombs ripping throughout your mouth, things that no longer hold their obvious appeal for me except on rare occasions), so what I tasted then would not be what I tasted now, an odd fact, but a true one. Today I bought this ironically, skeptically, whereas when I was ten this was *all* I wanted. This couldn't really be any good, could it? What's at stake for me here? Most things I remember being good in childhood seem to suck now (*The Dark Crystal,* Funyuns, Runts candy, Big League Chew). Will I be betrayed or be transported? I open my mouth, put a small piece in, and wait for wonder, miracle, the results.

Though I should add I am no less retarded about the problem of wanting my Wikipedia page, and wanting it to be accurate, wanting to tell my story, to reenact my drama and simulate it in your brain, wanting to read my story in others. I find it irksome and entertaining in almost equal measure. I don't read memoirs typically but I'm in the middle of a really interesting one, *Collections of Nothing*, by William Davies King, about his obsessive collections of ephemera—real ephemera in that they had no value at the time of their collection, and they have none now, and will not in the future: they are detritus and then they disappear. Except in this case they have not disappeared. King kept them, kept all of it (every box of cereal he ever ate, for instance, or the patterns on the linings of security envelopes, the stuff no one else would think to keep). What I like about it is its obsessiveness with the self, which mirrors the obsessiveness that the book[†] describes, so it applies its own methods to the self (and to the writing of the book, so it goes more than a little bit meta). And so at least I understand its methods, and can see its flaws. The technique—that self-obsession, that inclination for self-laceration, that way of mimicking the recursive nature of actual thought—also becomes annoying ("but it knows it's annoying," the writer might retort, but that doesn't make it less annoying), a too-familiar song lodged unwillingly in the brain, a jerk of the knee, a lack of more interesting and fruitful thinking. I want to edit it out even as I recognize it as something true. Some true things are not dramatic. But the minutiae of our existences are. These are facts, friends, all twenty thousand boxes of our lives of eating them. We are surrounded by their ordinary glory.

WELL THAT'S ONE THING WE GOT

The thing I love—the thing I presume everybody loves—about YouTube is its ability to provide, and continue providing, via associative clickable link and video response, completely guileless amateur entertainment. In some ways it is the antidote to craft, to the problem with memoir, in that craftlessness, the DIY ethic, is part of its raison d'être, part of what makes it tick, what makes it seem so real and immediate. It's you and the tube, not even a hyphen separating the two.

My experience, like so many modern experiences, starts with a forwarded email, with a link to an a cappella version of a catastrophically uninspired song, "Breakfast at Tiffany's," by the band Deep Blue Something, performed a cappella by the Dynamics from the University of Massachusetts ("UMass's hottest Acappella group"). It's a spectacular clip, featuring what appears to be twelve (you can't quite tell from the camera angle) college-age singers performing the song. What's great about it is what's great about a cappella groups and YouTube.com: no guile, an entirety of enthusiasm, a ball of yes, right on, and college try. I was in choir so I know these things quite well indeed. One guy, semi-nattily dressed, sings the lead, and the rest sing backup with a lot of doos and dahs. I can't tell if it's a concert clip or not, though they appear to be on a stage. They are having a great time. There is no irony. The dork factor is incredibly high, but the performance is so finely done it's hard to complain. Below the video there are 229 comments, including "good effort. love rhythmic effort by big lad on right" (one hour ago—!—considering the video was added on April 21, 2007) and "look how freeky [*sic*—as if we ever need to say *sic* in our reproductions of Internet commentary, which carries its own presumptions—however loaded—of ineptitude and the poor mechanics of the language of the same youth we log onto the Internet to watch and read about—their shocking sex habits (ooh!), their lackluster attention to the minutiae of grammar (oh!), their immensely revelatory blogs and drinking photos, their individuality, their failure to pay for recorded music—how we love to watch them, and this is directed at the youth, too, those twenty-two-year-olds I talked to last week lamenting the eighteen-year-olds' lack of modesty and their never not knowing the Internet; this youth-watching, this exasperated, entertained tut-tutting, is an inclusive sport] the big guy is dancing on the right." The big guy on the right is rocking, certainly, and he reminds me a little of my friend Mike, if Mike was ever in choir (doubtful, though he did appear in the choir photo in the yearbook[†] his senior year; he insinuated himself into a dozen group photos on photo day, just showing up and assembling when called, trying on successive identities: Speech Club Mike, Drama Club Mike, Choir Mike, Track and Field Mike, Drummer Mike, Dumber Mike, Soccer Mike, Wine Spectator Mike), or more likely myself. The lighting reminds me of, what, prom, which is still somehow short for *promenade,* and which is still tied to the idea of the promenade ball, with everyone posing for airbrushed photos in their rented limos or their parents' embarrassing cars, and living up to dorky ceremonial expectations?

The choir girls in the video are hot as they dance crappily.

Everyone seems so nice.

Two-thirds of the way through one of the girls comes out to duet and dance with the male lead. Shortly thereafter they break into "Moon River" instead of trying to otherwise represent the obligatory guitar solo and bridge. This is more than a little cheeky and referential, though charmingly so, and after that the dancers begin to really freak out. This is the stellar part, where it really gets good, the apex of the clip, though the film (if that's the word, if that doesn't imply too much production and premeditation, an auteur and script and art and more) cuts out before the applause might have cascaded through the space[†] in which they sing. The performance energy and the camera imply an audience, even if we don't see or hear it, and the harmony and arrangement on this version are strong, even if a little hilarious when watched out of context. I'm sure the live performance would be surprising and exhilarating, probably engaging the amusement response and the incredulity response, and finally the emotional response, among others. Put simply, this version blows the original out of the water. The song is stripped of its idiotic guitar sound and the bouncy '90s production and what I remember as everyone's terrible haircuts in the video (oh for the days[†] when songs were paired with videos—now videos, commercials, television shows are scored with songs). The UMass Dynamics' version has immediacy, expression, and excitement. They are really into it! They are taking this song to its maximum emotional effect! They are adorning it with exclamation points! And I can understand why people might have once found this song exciting and Why This Is Still Good.

An added dimension of Why This Is Good can be seen when comparing a performance like this to one, say, by the German cock rock band The Scorpions, you know, "Rock Me Like a Hurricane," being really their only *major* song, the only one that we can really count for anything in the long run (sorry, "Winds of Change," Wikipedia footnote about to be demoted to a former, abandoned draft), and the only major part of it being the chorus that you can summon immediately, unlike the rest of the song, if there is even a rest of the song, if there is anything in the darkness around us past the edge of memory[†] or vision. Their Scorpions' official website[†] has a 6,868-word essay that sits as the biography section. It makes a case (at length) for why they are an essentially important, monumental, always-to-be-capitalized rock band, including adjective-rich nuggets like "The distinctive SCORPIONS style came from the combination of two electric guitars, a fusion of fabulously forceful power riffs with dazzlingly exuberant guitar solos"; "To US audiences, the SCORPIONS, with their polished, hard-edged 'melodic rock' and Klaus Meine's dramatic power singing with its dizzying top notes, came to epitomise the best in heavy rock"; "By now the SCORPIONS were a household name"; "The SCORPIONS are still given a rapturous reception in Russia today"; "*Crazy World* is impressive testimony to the songwriting talents of the SCORPIONS' masterminds"; "The Hanover EXPO, June 22nd 2000. It was the 'Night of Nights,' the 'Battle of the Giants,' a 'musical exchange of fire' between rock band and classical orchestra of a standard never heard before." To this end, "[Conductor] Kolonovits achieved the ultimate fusion of these musical antitheses with Crossfire and the Deadly Sting Suite." It's hard for me to stop quoting this in the same way I can barely cease watching the YouTube clip we are discussing—both cascade charmingly and continue to expand throughout the virtual or other world. I'll include a few more: "The SCORPIONS had mastered the technique of unplugged playing"; "Rock music is their vocation, a tenet of their absolute professionalism"; "We've often been through hell, to experience heaven" (according to their founder, Rudolf Schenker). You can see the intern—though I prefer to think about this document as being produced in third person by the band itself, sitting around in their sweet leather pants after a concert, wheezing—really getting into this. It's the royal we, the immense machine of privilege that is the Scorpions, speaking into you from the void.

I particularly enjoy the rampant capitalization of SCORPIONS, leaving no doubt of their self-regard (hello, solipsism!), and as I have serious doubts that Germany is a habitat that supports scorpions, the whole idea of the band is a myth. The bio reads essentially like a press release for their new album, *Unbreakable*, like the comb, or like musician R. Kelly. Their music is "Music that satisfies the band's own musical needs and those of their audiences." Klaus Meine, vocalist (not to call him anything as banal as *singer*) for the Scorpions, says: "There'll never be any substitute for live concerts with real music and real feelings," which gives the live clip of "Breakfast" its real zing: real music, real feelings, real realness. Not live, but captured live, rehearsed, but not to the point of deadness, an effective and acceptable sense of being there. Charming youth. Our own lost, once charming youth. Were we lost? Were we ever charming? Were we even young?

The UMass Dynamics' performance is not the only version of this song on YouTube. There are versions on the site by the Accafellas and the Latonics, both all-male revues, which come complete with irony, antics, and a giggling cameraman. They are less engaging. Also one by the Kopitonez ("the only Asian-interest a cappella group at the University of Michigan"). In the comments section for the Kopitonez's clip a commenter complains that this is the Rockapella (best known for their theme song to the television game show *Where in the World Is Carmen Sandiego?*, based on the educational computer game that was maybe the only educational computer game ever to be a little bit fun) arrangement of the song, which might explain some of the viral nature of this particular song being performed by so many groups. The linkability of YouTube contributes to this too, since some people come for the song, others for the Dynamics or the

Kopitonez, and then you can immediately click over to other performances of it, working associatively.

The comments section is a key component of the experiencing of the clip. The audience for these clips is surely primarily people involved in other choirs or a cappella groups, or recovering members of the same. Perhaps some Deep Blue Something fans (Are there any? Reader, are you one? Would you stand up for DBS and their musical oeuvre?) find their way here and, incredulous, email the link to their friends: *you've gotta check this shit out*, if DBS fans or anyone else says *shit* anymore, if shockingly the swear words manage to live on and not fade away, probably because they have been proscribed and prohibited for most of our lives, so they retain their dangerous power, are passed from generation to generation like a secret. And so the thing spreads. At this point the video has 95,195 views,[1] which is still tiny fingerling potatoes by YouTube standards. At least twenty of these views are by me, I think, though the software can presumably filter out repeated viewings (perhaps the *views* statistic is views by different viewers, not the actual act of someone viewing the clip). If DBS the band itself actually came out against a cappella performances of the song and tried to have them squashed or legally blocked you could bet that, like *shit,* the video's audience would increase exponentially.

Yet other iterations on the site are by the Burlingtones, Men in Drag (University of Chicago), the Williams College Ephlats (initially a joyless performance, building a bit as they go, featuring a guy who is a dead ringer for a guy I knew in high school), the Drexel Doctor's Note (performing in a cathedral), BEATS (from the Raffles Institution, Singapore), 54th and City (Saint Joseph's University), a nearly unwatchable middle-school talent show (?) clip, the Rutgers Kol Halayla, the Sirens, and the list goes on and on. The muchness that the world—as encapsulated in YouTube, which must only show a sliver of the available versions or performances of this

---

[1] Since my original bender of clip watching, another 151,658 people have watched this clip. The number of comments has doubled. I am mentioned in a couple of comments since I read this essay a few times and underestimated my audience's ability to go online (probably in the very moment of listening to the essay, on their iPhone or whatever) and contribute to the conversation. The enthusiasm and skill of the Dynamics somehow continue to short-circuit the ironic response, the initial response to YouTube clips apparently being to laud or mock. One of the commenters, "Comedian618," sums it up well: "Not even I can make fun of this."

singularly forgettable pop song done variously charmingly a cappella—
offers us here is almost too much to take.

The shared culture of this song is great. Someone picked it up from
the dustbin of one-hit wonders and rehabilitated it (Rockapella, it would
seem), and the joy has spread. The song is liberated from its original, terrible context as the production of this band, and is growing through live
performance by amateurs (and, apparently, professionals). I haven't seen
any covers of it yet show up ironically on metal albums (though if you want
a great, almost-ironic cover, check out the version of "Don't You (Forget
About Me)," the most popular Simple Minds single in the United States, by
the metal band Life of Agony: their version actually really does the song
right, proves it's a great anthem; I imagine they took it on as a laugh, but
it became a serious performance as they found themselves inside it, perhaps in the way that these a cappella groups have done).² The song is, increasingly, one thing we got, a thing I got and gave up, a thing you are in
the process of getting, and a thing clearly got by a lot of a cappella groups,
mostly based in colleges, perhaps by you, as a potential former member
of a college a cappella group, or maybe you're just someone who saw a
performance once and found it strange. Or you tried out but didn't make
the group, those snob bastards. Or disdained it (you snob bastard), as is
only right. There are a thousand of us on stage with the UMass Dynamics,
thousands after thousands of us, ghosts up on risers in the gymnasiums
where we used to sing, where we will once again cry out our hosannas at
the end of the world.

The lovely thing about the college a cappella group is that it is transitory, staffed differently year to year. This version of the UMass Dynamics
is the version I will remember. The singing of this song will likely come
back to the members of the UMass Dynamics for this performance years
down the road, like occasionally bits of the songs my college choir sang
return to me at unexpected times, whether it's bits of *Peter Grimes* by
Benjamin Britten or a crappy song called "Market Woman" by some anonymous songwriter, which we sang with great festivity, adopting/exploring/
colonizing/donning the robes of the implied ethnicity of its subject and
singer, or whatever (though I can't say that sort of role-playing was not

---

² And in the way that my friend Jon did when choosing this song as his first foray into
karaoke.⁺

both ridiculous as well as fun, harmless, really, I hope). The mind returns these things, floats them up off the incredibly dense chemical stack that is memory, surfacing them in response to who knows what stimulus, and then we are transported. I say we because it once again allies me with my college choir, many of the actual people of whom I am and was ambivalent about, though the shared experience (some might say the shared ritual humiliation, given some of the things we were asked to do—though this is better related at another time, perhaps in concert with my many tales of watching or contemplating being in show choirs, which is the worst) creates a *we*, a choir. We sing things, do things we would never venture alone (though the braver among us have). My college choir even has a yearly rehearsal and performance with all the choir alumni every homecoming that I have routinely skipped, even when I go through the experience of homecoming, which I cannot reasonably recommend, trying to re-create that we. And for some of the we, surely it works.

This weekend is homecoming at the University of Arizona, and alumni flock back to town to try to reconnect with former people and places and re-experience their former selves.[†] This must be role-playing too. I can barely stand the thought (much less the sight or the experience) of actually being that person again, being known as that person again. Thoughts of high school are even worse. But still there's something—a connection that the alumni association surely wants to encourage as quickly as possible—and so homecoming is big business, too. The proliferation of video records of who we used to be must also limit us, or maybe remind us and allow us to hold our former selves to our present hearts. When camcorders made their way into my uncle's family, every family gathering was accompanied by a recording, usually left to the kids because of their increasing technological sophistication and less bounded energy, that must have been increasingly wack. Does my uncle's family ever watch these hundreds of videos? I hope not. They are private, or shared within a family, and are doubtfully of any mass interest. Like the phenomenon of sex tapes or the series of nude photos a friend confessed that she took of herself in college because this was as good, she said, as she was ever going to look, and she wanted to remember that body, that self—maybe they provide a more contemporary way of prompting memory, of committing vulnerability, of keeping everyone from getting too uppity (look, that was you, a chump like the rest of us), of living in the past as we always do among the effervescent scents of the present.

So the college a cappella group is the ideal version of the a cappella group, a shared, nerdy, temporary experience that we can look back on or have evoked unbidden in dreams or daily life. It's popular at college age or younger, where it's possible to joyfully and unself-consciously (and as such even gracefully) inhabit a song like this and perform it reasonably well and execute our collective crappy dance moves instead of hoarding them in private. The professional a cappella group must be afraid of hamming it up (though the barbershop quartet is stuffed with ham) or being too ironic or cute, since they're balding, or thinking about balding, or sagging, or sadly shuffling back and forth cynically, synchronized, toward the grave, and they must rely on execution and the created and riveting dream experience of the art performance. A cappella—amateur especially—is like karaoke in its leveling, but takes more guts and skill (no accompaniment, no one to cover for you—though the group dynamic helps to buffer, gild, and embolden), and the payoff is resultingly larger, and it is properly less ironic. But the conflation of I and we, past and present, subject and object—white girls singing slave songs, black boys doing Bach, you singing "Market Woman" accidentally in the megamarket where you shop for allegedly organic produce—is the same. This experience is what the Inventure Group saturn ring young and hip dancing models photo is really trying to convey: youth, excitement, unself-consciousness, gloriousness, beauty, potential, energy: *the future,* perhaps with nude photos or snack food.

Which is all to say that really you don't need to go beyond the UMass Dynamics' version of the song, at least this version online fixed in time until it's taken down or forgotten. It is in its own way as large and capacious as a life, as a memoir, as the World's Largest Ball† of Paint, both metaphor and thing. It is ring after ring of glistening meaning. It continues to give and grow. The Inventure Group would surely like to license it. The Inventure Group cannot ever license it, much less possess it, much less emulate, produce, tap into it, or pretend to comprehend it. This is what makes it good.

ASSEMBLOIR†: ENDING MEDITATION

Almost four decades have passed since this book† was lived.

I had spent the past thirty-nine months in army hospitals. I was ready to reclaim the years I'd lost and get on with my life.

My task here terminates. I have written of the immortal poet, and the man alike loveable and admirable, with one all-dominating desire—that of stating the exact truth, as far as I can ascertain or infer it, whatever may be its bearing.

I hope the Kuomintang will always be vigorous, dynamic, zealous, unselfish, having a new, fresh spirit. . . . Indeed, let us all work hard and together with tolerance, patience, and persistence. Let all Chinese be united, let us not act as a sheet of sand. Let us march forward. Let us welcome the challenge of the twenty-first century. Let us be fully prepared. Tears fall from my eyes.

We sat on the curb and looked up at two dark windows. I told Linda how a black friend had carried me to the bathroom the first day I had come home from the hospital, after she had been born. I'll leave us there, sitting close together on the curb. Now and then someone passed by but paid no attention to us as we told each other stories from our lives, falling silent every so often.

In the flickering chapel, the therapist plays "Silent Night, Holy Night" on the piano, and Susan and Janet, seated on either side of me, start to cry. I

Nothing is as pleasing as an end. Not beginnings, certainly, though they have their own pleasures, that of mystery and potential energy, the unknown. They give shape, surely, but ends define the shape. They close us down. They start to push us back out of our mothers'[†] warm and soothing laps. They suggest our own ends, our private dooms. Yet they are the same, mostly. We attenuate. We decay. We decease. Books end. And because of that dwindling space[†] we are more open to grandness than we might be otherwise. It is beautiful, to look back, to survey the territory covered, to conclude.

get a lump in my throat and hastily blow out my candle, splashing hot wax on my dress. Susan looks at me with a wet face and raised eyebrows. I give her a dirty look, and she turns away.

In that complex interplay of experience and physiology, I like to think that every time I gut it through and survive, I'm reshaping the structure and the chemistry of my thoughts, wearing new paths less tortured and convoluted than the old ones. Every new crisis successfully negotiated and survived inches me that much farther from the event horizon of despair.

I am most grateful to a woman named Mrs. Strange, my first foster mother, whom I have never had the chance to meet and thank, in whose home, in the first two years of my life, I learned to love pancakes.

And thou, sun, bright emblem of a far brighter effulgence, I bid farewell to thee also! I do not now take my last look of thee, for to thy glorious orb shall a poor suicide's last earthly look be raised. But, ah! who is yon that I see approaching furiously—his stern face blackened with horrid despair! My hour is at hand.—Almighty God, what is this that I am about to do! The hour of repentance is past, and now my fate is inevitable. —Amen, for ever! I will now seal up my little book, and conceal it; and cursed be he who trieth to alter or amend!

We scatter Anthony's ashes in the ocean from the beach in front of his mother's house. I stay for two days[†] and then go home. The doorman gives me a package of Anthony's things from the hospital: his sneakers, his Swiss Army watch, his gold wedding band.

This is where the wards are now, where patients are treated with new medications, new ideas applied. I wish them luck, say a prayer for them. May they go home soon. May they not take drugs for long. May they have the courage to look inside and love themselves. May they learn to feel at home in the world.

I set my candle on the pew beside me and dig my fingernails into their grooves, staring in silence at the wooden cross at the front of the chapel. You will not break me.

I understand at long last that this book is our imagined conversation, the intersection of the present and the past. I understand that what was missing could not be found in my parents' house, no longer my home, in that house empty of everything except memories; could not be found in Berkeley, in Cuba, not even here, in my present home, in New York; could

Maybe what memoirs offer us is another fiction: that of understanding. By reading memoir we can pretend to comprehend a life. Which means our lives have meaning, a thing that we might extract and present to God if and when we have the chance to do so. And if others can step back from their lives and can process them as stories, as effects with traceable causes and rising actions and epiphanies, then we are convinced we might also do so. We put down notes for our memoirs, for the books we're considering writing about our lives, or considering asking our distant relatives, or the women we meet on planes to write for us. I've got a story. It would make a great movie. Novel. Memoir.

only be found in my own being, the cells of my own body, my own mind. The threshold which takes real courage to cross. Not in retreat, barricaded, but going forward, recapturing meaning, wresting it from the violence that conceals it.

Play was stopped. The stadium seemed to shake. There was no doubt about it: the fans were going wild. And in that moment, as we pushed to our feet and opened our lungs and began to roar, my brothers and I were finally just like everybody else.

The night was still. The train started up soundlessly. After a few moments, we left the bridge and traveled on in the star-studded night toward the world where no one was waiting for us. In this moment—for the first time in my life—I really felt fear.[†] I realized I was free. I began to feel fear.

Thanks to God, we made it to Cadiz on the first of November, 1624. We disembarked and I remained for eight days, enjoying the hospitality of Señor don Fadrique de Toledo, who was general of the armada. As it turned out, two of my brothers were in his command and I became acquainted with them, and as an honor to me, a great honor, the general took one of them into his personal service and gave the other a promotion.

He was handsome and serious, bent over scripts in a hotel room, and then he stood and reached for my hand. Life will go on from here.

I never saw her again.

All of the anxiety and fear I had carried with me for thirty-nine years washed away in those first private moments, between this father and his son. Eli would have a home that he would want to come home to and never fear.

I have drawn the line, and I am still on this side of it.

One of the officers in this stateroom had a full case of liquor, a real pogue, fat and sleek and I could not figure how he carried the booze on board. He must have bribed people to help him. I began to think how we could get some of those bottles away from him. It would be a long voyage home, and it wasn't right that a rear-echelon pogue had all that liquor to himself.

And as I contemplate "The Juggler," my search for home, for myself, for that other who is also me, comes full circle.

This, then, is a map of my own making. This is the story I am learning to live.

I love this muchness of experience, though, the specificity, each moment of individual experience, rendered with panache, each element of et cetera, the awkward interactions, the fairies, the thorn trees, the technologies, the armadas, the gold wedding bands, the bitter winter days!—these things come without end, offered up by world, that Ball,[†] big gobstopper, stuck and decomposing in our universe-sized craw. Our mouths are propped open by it. How can we live without this seemingly endless choice? How can we live with this seemingly endless choice? Now that we can do anything, information and design theorist Bruce Mau asks us, what should we do? In the post-postmodern world, in the world starting to secede away from memoir, from the illusion of representation, and back toward memory,[†] an amateur project on the whole, it is hard not to be paralyzed. Maybe the Oulipo got it right: constraint enables. Let's make rules so we can follow them and then so we can break through them. By breaking through them we may start to feel alive again.

I follow the pallbearers down the aisle and sit silently in the pew at the front of the church.

No, there is no question about it this time—at long last, my viscera yield and concede: *I am back in the place† I never should have left.*

And now, dear reader, the time has come for you and me to part. Let us hope that it is not final. A traveler finds himself compelled to repeat the regretful parting word often. During the career recorded in the foregoing book, I have bidden many farewells: to the Wagogo, with their fierce effrontery; to Mionvu, whose blackmailing once so affected me; to the Wavinza, whose noisy clatter promised to provoke dire hostilities; to the inhospitable Warundi; to the Arab slave-traders and half-castes; to all fevers, remittent and intermittent; to the sloughs and swamps of Makata; to the brackish waters and howling wastes; to my own dusky friends and followers, and to the hero-traveller and Christian gentleman, David Livingstone. It is with kindliest wishes to all who have followed my footsteps on these pages that I repeat once more—Farewell.

I was at peace. I was home.

So I am wishing you love. Love that embraces you for who you are. Love that sees all of you and asks no sacrifice. Love that you can accept because you have loved yourself first.

Slowly, resentfully, I have moved out of slavery, though I cannot forget its freedom. But I am no longer blinded by obsession. I can now recognize what is commonly termed reality, wretched reality. I even live in it on occasion, when feeling perverse. I have endured the loss. Choice is mine. But I know what to do—and where to go—should I need a fix of beauty, of submission, of relief, of bliss. And, besides, I still have the Box. It does not only contain his DNA. It contains my very own madness—safely captured under its gilded lid.

But I don't need to open it. I have the key.

I want to thrive in the woods and die in the woods, return to the woods and become born in the woods.

We hummed louder, but when they picked up handfuls of leaves and twigs to throw at us, we stopped and mockingly opened our arms to them. Leaves fluttered in the air, and we chased them humming all the way down the hill to the car.

At a time like this, one must say farewell to the "I" bound to the native land.

Thinking about the memoir, or our lives at all, is thinking about death, about technology, about how obsolete we all are soon to become, and about our desire for preservation beyond the limits of the body. The floppy disk's life span was a dozen years, maybe. The CD's or DVD's physical persistence as readable data is probably a decade, depending on the quality of the physical media. The book's tenure is longer if printed on archival paper with the right sort of ink. The life story, the arc of narrative, the literary present tense, that state enabled by the representation of a consciousness,[†] far longer. The life span of the Presidential Museum,[†] the monument, the inexplicable obelisk, the Ball of Paint, is even longer still.

Finding the courage to tell my story, I have overcome my fear and replaced it with love.

In short, we must either conceive him not only the greatest fool, but the greatest wretch, on whom was ever stamped the form of humanity; or, that he was a religious maniac, who wrote and wrote about a deluded creature, till he arrived at that height of madness, that he believed himself the very object whom he had been all along describing. And, in order to escape from an ideal tormentor, committed that act for which, according to the tenets he embraced, there was no remission, and which consigned his memory and his name to everlasting detestation.

I want to stay home.

I am ready to leave.

Sometimes the asterisk is an open door, a gate, a star getting closer by the moment. The word *disaster* comes from the end of stars, the disappearance of the exterior world, and therefore, implicitly, our own. When the stars—or our ability to imagine ourselves among them, to find meaning in their patterns, to project our stories onto their apparent motions—end, we end too.

VANISHING POINT FOR SOLO VOICE

The laptop light dims my awareness of the outside world. It is far into the night in the middle of Ohio, and I am surrounded by communicating crickets. Steam or smoke towers from the power plant and trails directly west, a single strand over the campus of the College of Wooster, toward the once-American future.

This we has dwindled down to I. The court emptied. The stage bare. There is one light. There is a door. I am being introduced. What do I want to do?

For one, I'd like to find the courage not to tell my story. Since we would all—apparently—prefer to tell our stories, the smarter thing, the harder thing for lots of us, is silence. Or at least discretion. Restraint. I am just I here and the world does not need more of me. So what justification, this? To see my name in prose, in print, at length? It's therapeutic. I am an extrovert, entirely vertical with my back to the wall. No scoliosis here.

Half a day later and I am in airports, which might as well be the waiting room at the cancer doctor's, or outright purgatory. I am nowhere. I am nothing. I sit in the airport spelled DFW, and I wish it was after the recently departed David Foster Wallace. I've photographed a bunch of signs with DFW at their center. It is as if the whole word, nay, world, is summoned up for him in this place[†] of constant arrivals and departures. The place is new plastered over old, efficiency, complexity underpinned by history.

Everything depends on a technology in dire need of an overhaul: air traffic control, which seems almost to work well enough, which is to say that we are not aware of it except when we are circling Minneapolis waiting for our place in the queue to land. I fly United as often as I can because channel 9 on the in-air radio lets you listen in on cockpit communications with air traffic control. I am reminded of Orpheus in the Cocteau film *Orpheus*, listening to the other world through the radio, a technology that continually surprises and brings us something from seemingly nothing, even as we have become inured to it, accustomed to signals everywhere around us all the time, even as we have become used to being obliterated by information. Moments like these are rare enough, glimpsing something of the beyond. I am high above the world, and being privy to this undercarriage reassures me. I am not just I, I am one of many Is, many stories on the plane, crisscrossing thousands of other vectors, itineraries, plots for planes, all subject to adjustment by one of many air traffic control centers. I hear the frequencies switch, the air speeds, the vectors, the greetings, the commentaries on potential turbulence, light chop at this altitude, and can we move up a couple thousand feet. I can hear one controller give way to another, the breathless way one controller issues commands almost simultaneously to a dozen planes, and another's chatter subsumed by silence and the plane's beginning to bank toward another vector. I listen to the chatter, evidence of a human interaction, a life summoned up by just a voice. I am nowhere now. I am in the air. I am everywhere at once.

NOTES

This book was completed with the help of a Summer Research Stipend and a Research Grant-in-Aid from the Faculty Research and Development Center at Grand Valley State University.

Thanks to Wendy Sumner-Winter from the *Pinch* for her design hand on "Solipsism." Thanks to Adam Gopnik and Robert Atwan from *The Best American Essays*. Thanks, too, to Dinty Moore and Lee Gutkind from *Best Creative Nonfiction 2*. And thanks to Heidi Julavits for her conversation about the I and her excellent editorial eye.

Big thanks to Scott Moyers for his work and enthusiasm.

Text for the assembloirs here and on the website is collaged from the following memoirs:

Laurie Adler, *Until Tonight: A Memoir*
Joel Agee, *In the House of My Fear*
Kingsley Amis, *Memoirs*
Martin Amis, *Koba the Dread: Laughter and the Twenty Million*
Roger Angell, *Let Me Finish*
A. Manette Ansay, *Limbo*
Davar Ardalan, *My Name Is Iran*
Jimmy Santiago Baca, *A Place to Stand: The Making of a Poet*
Chet Baker, *As Though I Had Wings: The Lost Memoir*

Toni Bentley, *The Surrender*

Alfred Bercovici, *That Blackguard Burton! A Biography of Sir Richard Francis Burton, The Fabulous Lover, Daring Explorer, Prolific Author, Who Went Where He Pleased and Did What He Liked*

Judy Blunt, *Breaking Clean*

L. M. Boston, *Perverse and Foolish: A Memoir of Childhood and Youth*

James Brady, *The Coldest War*

Anthony Burgess, *You've Had Your Time: The Second Part of the Confessions*

Elinor Burkett, *So Many Enemies, So Little Time*

Nicolas de Basily, Diplomat of Imperial Russia, 1903–1917, *Memoirs*

Catalina de Erauso, Michele Stepto, Gabriel Stepto, *Lieutenant Nun*

Pete Dexter, *Paper Trails*

Joan Didion, *The Year of Magical Thinking*

John W. Dodds, *American Memoir*

Bob Dole, *One Soldier's Story*

Carlos Eire, *Waiting for Snow in Havana: Confessions of a Cuban Boy*

Wang Fan-hsi and Gregor Benton, *Memoirs of a Chinese Revolutionary*

Antwone Quenton Fisher, Mim Eichler Rivas, *Finding Fish*

Michael J. Fox, *Lucky Man: A Memoir*

Paula Fox, *Borrowed Finery*

Jonathan Franzen, *How to Be Alone*

Eileen J. Garrett, *Adventures in the Supernormal: A Personal Memoir*

Martha Gellhorn, *Travels with Myself and Another*

Graham Greene, *The Lawless Roads*

Edward T. Hall, *An Anthropology of Everyday Life*

Suheir Hammad, *Drops of This Story*

Peter Handke, *A Sorrow beyond Dreams*

Eddy L. Harris, *Still Life in Harlem*

Anne Heche, *Call Me Crazy*

Joseph Heller, *Now and Then: From Coney Island to Here*

Theodor Herzl, *The Diaries of Theodor Herzl*

James Hogg, Peter Garside, *The Private Memoirs and Confessions of a Justified Sinner*

Jeanne Wakatsuki Houston and James D. Houston, *Farewell to Manzanar*

Pico Iyer, *The Lady and the Monk*

LL Cool J with Karen Hunter, *I Make My Own Rules*

Peter Jenkins, *Along the Edge of America*

Caroline Kettlewell, *Skin Game*

Marvin Korman, *In My Father's Bakery: A Bronx Memoir*

Sir Harry Lauder, *Roamin' in the Gloamin'*

Christopher Kennedy Lawford, *Symptoms of Withdrawal*

Irving Lazar, *Swifty: My Life and Good Times*

Mindy Lewis, *Life Inside*

Ch'en Li-Fu, Sidney H. Chang, and Ramon Hawley Myers, *The Storm
Clouds Clear over China*

Betty Mahmoody with William Hoffer, *Not without My Daughter*

William Manchester, *Goodbye, Darkness: A Memoir of the Pacific War*

Hilary Mantel, *Giving Up the Ghost*

Sándor Márai, Albert Tezla, *Memoir of Hungary, 1944–1948*

Joyce Maynard, *Looking Back: A Chronicle of Growing Up Old in the Sixties*

Walter Dean Myers, *Bad Boy*

Bich Minh Nguyen, *Stealing Buddha's Dinner: A Memoir*

Chris Offutt, *No Heroes*

Molly O'Neill, *Mostly True*

Carole Radziwill, *What Remains: A Memoir of Fate, Friendship, and Love*

Hilton Howell Railey, *Touch'd with Madness*

Jacob A. Riis, *The Making of an American*

Victor Rivas Rivers, *A Private Family Matter*

John D. Rockefeller, *Random Reminiscences of Men and Events*

Richard Rodriguez, *Hunger of Memory: The Education of Richard
Rodriguez*

Anne Roiphe, *1185 Park Avenue: A Memoir*

William Michael Rossetti, *A Memoir of Shelley*

Lisa St. Aubin de Terán, *The Hacienda*

Margaret A. Salinger, *Dream Catcher*

Julia Scheeres, *Jesus Land*

Floyd Schmoe, *For Love of Some Islands*

John Sellers, *Perfect from Now On: How Indie Rock Saved My Life*

Susan Sherman, *America's Child: A Woman's Journey through the Radical
Sixties*

David Shields, *Enough about You: Adventures in Autobiography*

Charles Simic, *A Fly in the Soup*

Ted Solotaroff, *First Loves: A Memoir*

Gary Soto, *Living Up the Street*

Wole Soyinka, *You Must Set Forth at Dawn*
William Spratling, *File on Spratling: An Autobiography*
Henry M. Stanley, *How I Found Livingstone in Central Africa*
Peter Trachtenberg, *7 Tattoos: A Memoir in the Flesh*
Michael Tucker, *Living in a Foreign Language: A Memoir of Food, Wine, and Love in Italy*
Franz Wisner, *Honeymoon with My Brother: A Memoir*

Thanks particularly to Dolly Laninga, who scoured through memoirs with me for this project.

For "Well That's One Thing We Got," thanks to Mike Dombrowski for lending me his yearbook and his story.

And to Nicole Walker, for being one of the few people I like to read my work in progress, for making it suck somewhat less.

And to Katie Dublinski, for bearing with me. I should probably thank everyone for this.

Remember, you: other electricities.com/vp/ . . .

ACKNOWL-EDGMENTS

—"Ander Alert" originally appeared in the *Normal School*

—"Ceremony" originally appeared in the *Believer* and was reprinted in *The Best Creative Nonfiction 2*, edited by Lee Gutkind

—"The Essay Vanishes" appeared in *Indiana Review*

—"Exteriority" appeared in *Hotel Amerika*

—"Geas" appeared in *Fourth Genre*

—"Solipsism," originally published on my website, was republished in the *Pinch*, and was later reprinted in *The Best American Essays 2008*, edited by Adam Gopnik

—"Voir Dire" originally appeared in the *Believer*

Ander Monson is the author of *Neck Deep and Other Predicaments,* winner of the Graywolf Press Nonfiction Prize; the novel *Other Electricities;* and the poetry collections *Vacationland* and *The Available World.* He lives and teaches in Arizona and edits the magazine *DIAGRAM* (thediagram.com) and the New Michigan Press. Find him and his work online at otherelectricities.com.

Composition by BookMobile Design and Publishing Services, Minneapolis, Minnesota. Manufactured by Versa Press on acid-free paper.